made for baby

Cute Sewn Gifts

Ayda Algın

TUVA

FABRIC BUTTONS

Tuva Publishing

www.tuvapublishing.com

Address Merkez Mah. Cavusbasi Cad. No:71
Cekmekoy - Istanbul 34782 / Turkey
Tel: +9 0216 642 62 62

Made For Baby

First Print 2017 / March

All Global Copyrights Belong To
Tuva Tekstil ve Yayıncılık Ltd.

Content Sewing

Editor in Chief Ayhan DEMİRPEHLİVAN
Project Editor Kader DEMİRPEHLİVAN
Designer Ayda ALGIN
Technical Editors Sedef IMER, Leyla ARAS, Büşra ESER
Graphic Designers Ömer ALP, Abdullah BAYRAKÇI
Assistant Zilal ÖNEL
Photography Tuva Yayıncılık, Ayda ALGIN
Illustrations Murat Tanhu YILMAZ

ISBN: 978-605-9192-11-8

Printing House
Bilnet Matbaacılık ve Ambalaj San. A.Ş.

 TuvaYayincilik  TuvaPublishing

 TuvaYayincilik TuvaPublishing

introduction

Growing up I loved dolls - I still do to this day! I literally played house until high school. I loved dolls so much that I'd sleep with them; I'd dream of dresses I'd sew for them. The fabrics left over from my mother's dresses were my inspiration and my most valued treasures.

My mother is an excellent dressmaker. She'd sew such amazing dresses for my sister and I - I still remember most of them! Although I never touched my mother's sewing machine at the time, I'm almost certain that my inclination, curiosity and love towards hand crafts is her legacy. I should also mention my paternal aunts; they are two of the most skillful and creative women I've ever known.

I left my family at the age of 18 and moved to Istanbul for university. For the following few years my heavy work schedule left no time for hobbies, until 2011. With a reduced business workload I found time for myself and my hobbies and discovered a new world. I first started my blog: cafenoHut, where I shared my favourite hand crafts, home decoration ideas and tried and tested recipes. I was so thrilled to share my fun creations and love of crafts with the world. The more I shared the more I learnt. My love of crafts just kept growing as I saw the happiness my creations brought to my own world, and everyone around me.

That year, my sister gave me a sewing machine for my birthday, which kickstarted my sewing adventure. It sat untouched for a week! That weekend I I finally sat at the machine, just because I didn't want to dissapoint my sister. I had never imagined sewing could be this fun!

I have no formal sewing training - I just developed my own methods, watched tons of videos, got inspired by many talented sewing bloggers, made and continue to make mistakes. I'm still learning and for me that's the best part!

I love sewing things for babies and gifting beautiful items to my friends. A new baby's arrival is a great cause for celebration and a great opportunity to prepare handmade gifts. In a consumer world where buying things is the norm, gifts made by hand and with love are all the more cherished and treasured.

This book contains projects either for your lovely baby or the baby of a loved one. The projects are simple and cute, and can be made quickly with both ease and pleasure. This book contains the basics for beginner sewers and loads of fun ideas for the experienced. I hope you like it!

Ayda Algın

Contents

Sewing Essentials

A sewing machine alone is not enough to sew. Without the correct tools, even professional sewists can not obtain good results. Pay particular attention to quality when choosing your sewing tools. Once you are well equipped you too will see how everything becomes easier and more enjoyable! All tools listed below can be obtained from haberdashery or various online stores:

1. Cutting mat
2. Rotary cutter
3. Quilting ruler
4. Fabric glue
5. Heat-erasable or water-erasable fabric pen
6. Needles and pins
7. Fusible web
8. Basting spray
9. Tailor's chalk
10. Scissors
11. Embroidery hoop
12. Tape measure
13. Seam ripper
14. Iron

Techniques

CLAMSHELL APPLIQUE WITH ENGLISH PAPER PIECING

SEA SHELL

1 Copy the clamshell template from the 'Templates' section at the back onto card stock or heavy weight paper to make as many clamshell paper pieces as required for your project.

2 Place a clamshell paper piece on the wrong side of the fabric, and cut all the way around with an allowance of ¼" (0.6 cm) to ⅜" (1 cm).

3 Apply the fabric glue on the long curve of the paper piece, fold the fabric towards it finger-pressing the curved edge.

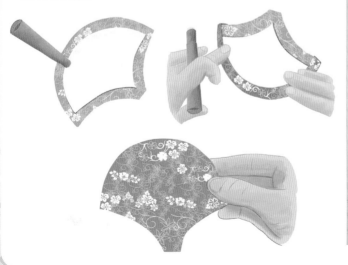

4 Prepare as many clamshells as required for you project. To join two clamshells, place them right sides together aligning the edges. Fasten these tw pieces with 3 tiny whip-stitches (approximately 1 mr apart) from the starting point of the long curved edg being careful to use a thin, threaded needle with matching color so that the stitches do not show on th right side.

5 You will need a backing fabric to fix the first line clamshells. Backing fabric should be bigger tha the finished clamshell line by around ½" (1.3 cm) on th right and left; and 1" (2.5 cm) on the top and bottor edges.

6 Fold the backing fabric lengthways and press t mark a crease. This will be the border for the to of the clamshells.

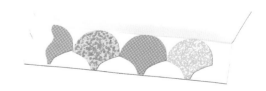

7 Carefully remove the paper pieces from the clamshells. Put small dots of fabric glue on the curved edges (you can also use a thin brush to apply the glue).

8 Place the first line of clamshells, using the crease as a guide for the top border, press with hot iron to fasten them to the backing fabric and fix the clamshells to the fabric with tiny applique stitches approximately 2-3 mm apart along the curved edges.

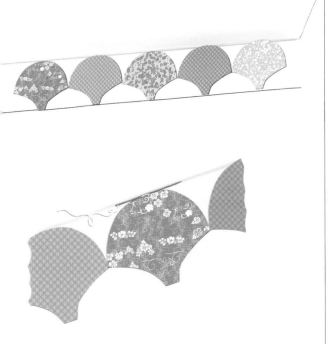

9 Prepare the second line of clamshells in the same manner. After applying the fabric glue, place the second line of clamshells onto the first line, aligning their long curved edge with the joining point of two clamshells on the first line as shown in the picture. Fasten the second line of clamshells to the first line with applique stitch. Repeat these steps as many times as your project requires.

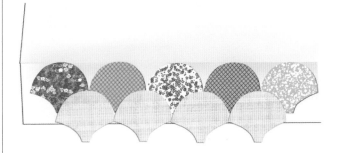

MAKING A BIAS TAPE

Bias binding is used for several projects in this book. This technique gives a professional and clean finished look to your projects.

For binding you can either use a double-folded store-bought bias tape or make your own according to the below instructions.

1 Cut diagonal strips from the fabric measuring 4 times wider than the bias tape you want to make and join them as shown in the drawing.

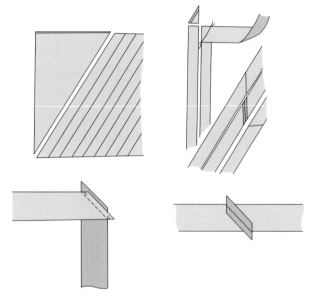

2 Press the joined strips, fold in half lengthways, press again to obtain a crease. Open the crease and fold the outside edges towards it so that they in the middle (as shown in the drawing); press again. Your bias tape is ready to use.

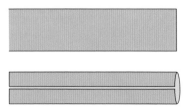

BIAS BINDING

1 Open the ready-to-use double-folded bias tape tha you have bought or made. Pin the bias tape to th fabric right sides together, with raw edges aligned. Se with a ¼" (0.5 cm) seam allowance.

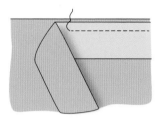

2 To turn the corners, fold the bias tape up at a 9 degree angle aligning the raw edges and fold again backwards as shown in the drawing.

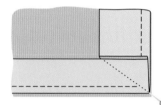

3 When you come back to the starting point, leav a seam allowance that is equal to the bias tap width and cut the excess fabric. Align the raw ends the bias tape up at a 90 degree angle, draw a 45 degre diagonal line to join them and sew along this line. Cu off excess fabric ¼" (0.5 cm) away from the seam. Yo can also join the ends flat instead of diagonal. Press th seam open, and finish sewing the bias tape in place.

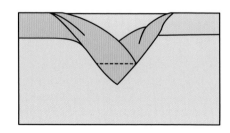

4 Fold the bias tape sewn to the right side of the fabric over the edge, to the back of the fabric and applique stitch to fasten. At the corners, fold the tape backwards. Continue stitching as you form a mitred corner.

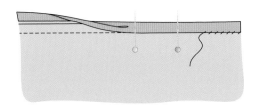

QUILTING

1 Preparing the quilt top: This usually involves patchwork (may also be the outer part of a blanket, table-runner or pillowcase). Once finished, the quilt top must be ironed flat.

2 Preparing the quilt sandwich: This is composed of three layers: quilt top (as above), quilt batting and backing (or lining) fabric. If made for baby, you may prefer a quilt batting made of natural materials like cotton.

To fasten the three layers together you can use curved quilters pins or a basting spray. I prefer basting spray to avoid bulk forming between the layers.

To Spray Baste: lay the batting on a protected surface and place the backing fabric on top, right side facing up. Fold up half of the backing fabric, spray the basting spray on the batting and then lay the fabric back down carefully. Smooth out any wrinkles with your hands. Repeat the same process for the other half; folding up, spray the adhesive, lay the fabric back down and smooth the surface.

3 Quilting: Quilting is the process of sewing these three layers (quilt top, batting and backing) to each other. It can be done by hand or with a sewing machine. For the projects in this book, hand quilting is used for the nostalgic touch it gives the finished item.

If you use hand quilting, always bury your knots: give the thread a tug until the knot passes through the backing fabric and remains buried in the batting layer, so it doesn't show on either side of the quilt.

4 Bias Binding: the last and the finishing step in quilting. You can refer to the "bias binding" section for details.

RAW EDGE APPLIQUE

TIP: If you use a dark color thread when sewing around the appliques, the edges will be more prounounced. If you sew twice around the appliques, the thread will show more and the edges will be more secure.

1 Copy the applique patterns onto cardstock and cut them out to prepare your templates. Place the template on the paper backing of the fusible web and trace around with a pencil.

2 Cut around the template leaving a ¼"(6 mm) seam allowance. Place the adhesive side of the fusible web to the wrong side of the fabric that you will use for the applique and press with hot iron for 5-10 seconds. Repeat this process for all applique pieces.

3 Cut out the pieces on the traced pencil lines.

4 Peel off the paper backing and place the appliques on the background fabric. Make sure that the pieces which are meant to touch each other slightly overlap, and that the order of the pieces are correct before pressing. Fuse the applique pieces to the background fabric by pressing with an iron for around 5-10 seconds on each applique. Do not move the iron while pressing as this may distort the pieces.

5 Machine stitch around the edges of each applique twice with short stitches and sewing as close to the edges as possible (1-2 mm). Use a dark color thread for a more distinct effect and a light color thread for a less visible result.

MAKING A TASSEL

1 Cut a cardboard to the length that you wish your fringes to measure.

2 Wrap the yarn around it until you reach the desired thickness.

3 Pass a piece of yarn, folded in half, under the wrapped yard on the cardboard, making a tight knot at the top.

4 Slide wrapped yarn off the cardboard and tie another piece of yarn around the top of the tassel tightly as shown in the picture.

5 Trim tassel ends to even their lengths.

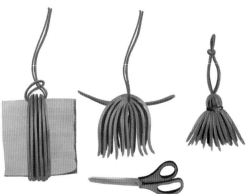

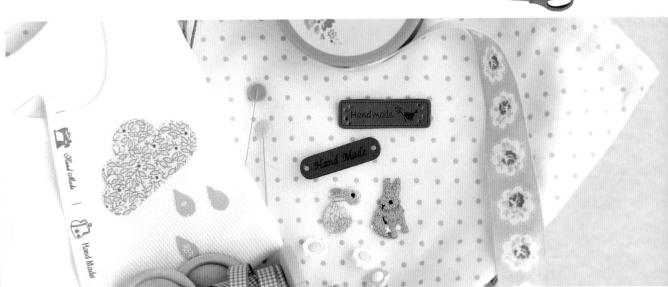

Hand Stitches

UNNING STITCH

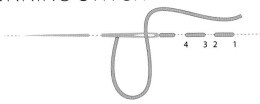

ES Outlining, straight and curved lines, hand quilting.

ork from right to left.

ng thread up at 1 then down at 2, up at 3 and down
4 and continue. The spaces between the stitches
be the same length as the stitches or shorter for a
erent look.

PS
ep an even tension and avoid pulling thread or the
ches will pucker.

VHIP STITCH

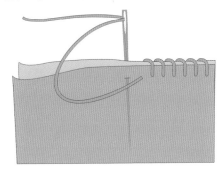

e whipstitch is probably the fastest and easiest stitch to
e when hand sewing. It's a good all-purpose stitch and
orks well for most puppet building fabrics (ie. various
eces and fur).

th the right sides of the fabric together, push your threaded
edle into the wrong side of one of the pieces of fabric,
rough the second piece of fabric, so that it comes out the
ong side of the second piece. Loop the needle around
er the top of where the two pieces come together and
ain push the needle into the wrong side of the first piece
fabric, through the second, and out. Continue to stitch in
is manner for the length of the seam.

BACK STITCH

USES Outlining, straight and curved lines.

Work from right to left.
Bring needle up at 1 and back down at 2.
Move left and bring needle up at 3, then back down at 1.
Continue stitching.

TIPS
Make shorter stitches for curved lines and shapes.

LADDER STITCH

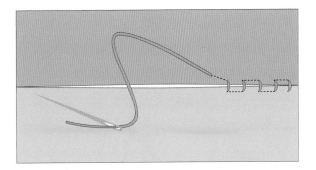

An invisible stitch used to sew two folded edges
together. Moving from right to left, take a small stitch
out of one side of the folded edge, then move forward
and take a small stitch out of the other side. Every so
often, pull the thread taut, so that the fabric edges
close and the stitches vanish.

CROSS STITCH

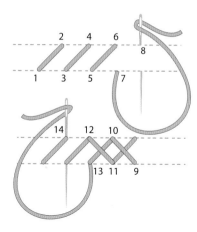

USES Borders and filling if worked in adjacent rows.

To stitch a line: Stitching from left to right, bring needle up at 1, down at 2, then up at 3 and down at 4. Continue stitching across to end of line.
Start back stitching from right to left, make crosses by bringing the needle up at 9 and down at 10. Continue until all crosses have been stitched.

TIPS
Be sure to keep the top stitch on the cross the same direction throughout a project.

STRAIGHT STITCH

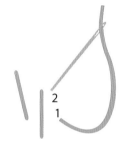

To work this simple stitch bring your needle up at 1 and down at 2 to complete the stitch.

SATIN STITCH

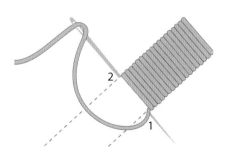

USES Solid filling for shapes, great for monograms

Bring needle up at 1, down at 2, then back up right next to 1 and down right next to 2. Place stitches close together to fill in area. Be sure the thread lays flat and without any twisting to produce a smooth look.

TIPS
To raise the stitching, back-stitch just inside the outline of the shape before starting.

FRENCH KNOT

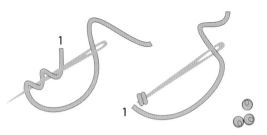

Uses: Decorative dots, filling flower centers, leaves, plants, eyes.

Bring needle up at 1.
Hold thread taut with other hand and wrap the thread twice around end of the needle.
Gently pull the thread so that the wrapped thread

ghten and while holding it taut, insert the needle next
1. Pull thread through onto the backside until the knot
formed and lies securely on the surface.

PS
make a larger knot, wrap the thread around the
eedle a couple of extra times or use a thicker thread.

BLANKET STITCH

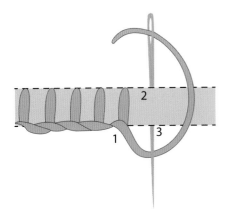

SES Straight and gently curved lines, borders and
nishing edges.

Vork from left to right.
ring needle up at 1, down at 2 and up at 3, keeping
he thread looped under the needle.
ull thread through and shape the stitch as desired.
epeat multiple stitches until complete.

IPS
or an even line of stitching keep the height of the
titches even throughout.
o vary the look of the stitch, change the height of
ach stitch making one long and one short.

Projects

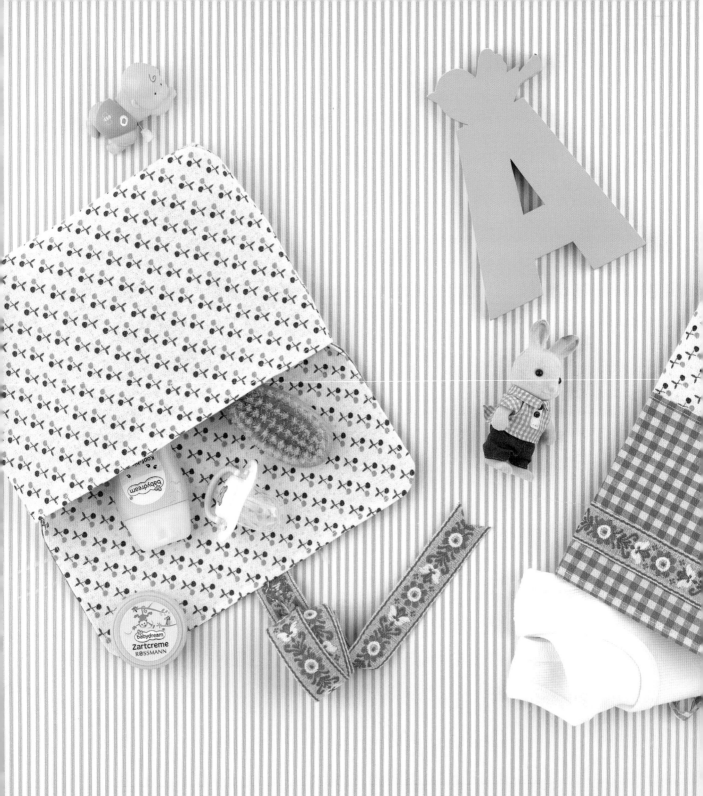

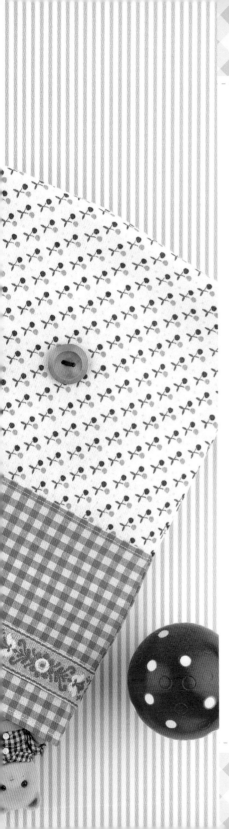

Travel Set

Taking your baby on an outing requires planning ahead. You should be well prepared to have all the necessities for when you need to feed, change or calm your baby.

I had this in mind while designing this travel set. You can sew this two piece set for your own baby or to gift. Perfect for carrying all essential baby gear!

FINISHED MEASUREMENTS
SMALL BAG WITH RIBBON ⊕ 9″ x 6 ¼″ (23 x 16 cm)
FABRIC BAG WITH PLASTIC LINING ⊕ 8 ½″ x 11 ¾″ (22 x 30 cm)

MATERIALS

FOR THE SMALL BAG WITH RIBBON

⊕ 9 ¾" x 13 ¾" (25 x 35 cm) cotton fabric for the bag outer

⊕ 9 ¾" x 13 ¾" (25 x 35 cm) cotton fabric for the lining

⊕ 9 ¾" x 13 ¾" (25 x 35 cm) medium weight fusible interfacing

⊕ 2 pieces of 9 ¾" x 5" (25 x 13 cm) cotton fabric for the flap

⊕ 9 ¾" x 5" (25 x 13 cm) fusible interfacing for the flap

⊕ ¾" (2.5 cm) wide, 32 ¼" (82 cm) long, decorative ribbon

⊕ Cute wooden button (optional)

FOR THE FABRIC BAG WITH PLASTIC LINING

⊕ 2 pieces of 9 ½" x 7 ¾" (24 x 20 cm) cotton fabric for the bottom part of the bag (B)

⊕ 2 pieces of 9 ½" x 5 ½" (24 x 14 cm) cotton fabric for the upper part of the bag (A)

⊕ 2 pieces of 9 ½" x 2 ¼" (24 x 5.5 cm) cotton fabric for the ining (C)

⊕ 2 pieces of 9 ½" x 11 ¼" (24 x 28.5 cm) oven roasting bag for the lining (D)

⊕ 2 pieces of 1" (2.5 cm) wide, 9 ½" (24 cm) long, decorative ribbon

⊕ 1 ¼" x 4 ¾" (3 x 12 cm) cotton fabric for the button loop

⊕ Wooden button

INSTRUCTIONS FOR THE SMALL BAG WITH RIBBON

1 Fuse the interfacing to the wrong side of the oute fabric, aligning all edges. Fold the fabric in half right sid facing together and sew the short edges together on bot sides. Press seams open. Fold the bottom seam over th side seam so that it forms a triangle and the side seam centered as shown in the drawing, measure ¾" (2 cm) fron the triangle's peak across the bottom seam and mark it a the middle point. Draw a ¾" (2 cm) line from the middl point both to the right and to the left (total 1 ½" (4 cm)) an sew along this line back-tacking at each end of the stitch lin (you can sew twice across the line to reinforce the stitching Cut the excess fabric ⅜" (1 cm) away from the seam. Repea for the other corner. Turn right side out.

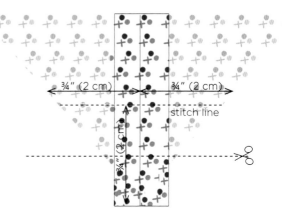

¾" (2 cm)   ¾" (2 cm)

stitch line

2 Repeat Step 1 to prepare the lining of the bag bu this time without interfacing. While sewing the shor edges together, leave a 2 ¾" (7 cm) opening at one side fo turning. Don't turn the lining right side out, leave as sewn

3 Fuse the interfacing to the wrong side of the fabric fo the flap outer, aligning all edges. Place on a flat surfac right side of fabric facing up. Position the ribbon on top, righ side facing up, on the centre of one long edge of the fla outer, with the raw edge of ribbon aligned with the raw edg of fabric. Baste the ribbon in place by hand or by machin ⅛" (0.3 cm) away from the edge.

4 Lay the flap's inner piece and outer piece (that yo sewed the ribbon to) right sides facing together. A

hown in the drawing, draw a curve on both corners of
he long edge where the ribbon end is sewn and sew
round the three edges of the flap with a ⅜" (1 cm) seam
llowance, leaving one long edge unsewn (this will remain
the bag). Turn right side out, and press. Top stitch the 3
ewn sides 2 mm from the edge.

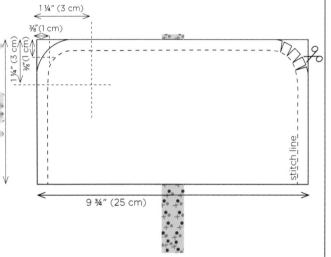

INSTRUCTIONS FOR THE FABRIC BAG
WITH PLASTIC LINING

1 Take one piece of ribbon and one piece of B fabric.
Place the ribbon parallel to one long edge the fabric
approximately 1 ½" (4cm) below the edge (right sides of
both ribbon and fabric facing up). Baste the ribbon to the
fabric across the two ends.

2 Repeat Step 1 to make one more.

3 Take a B piece from the previous step and place
right sides together against an A piece, long edge
of B aligned against the matching edge of A. Sew along
the length. Press the seam allowance towards B and top
stitch 2 mm next to the seam.

4 In the same way, sew the C piece to the B piece,
and the D piece to the C piece.

5 For the button loop, fold the loop fabric in half
lengthways (right side out), press to make a crease
and open. Fold the long raw edges inwards, meeting at
the crease in the middle. Fold in half again lengthways,
press and top-stitch the long edges.

6 Repeat steps 3 and 4 with the remaining A, B, C,
and D pieces. But this time, while joining the B and
C fabrics sandwich the button loop in between them at
the centre (raw edges aligned) and sew.

5 Place the bag's outer piece inside the lining,
right sides together. Place the flap between the
ag outer and the lining. Match the flap's raw edges:
ap's outer part placed against the bag outer, and
he ribbon flap edge pointing down. Sew all the way
long the top edge with a ⅜" (1 cm) seam allowance.
urn the bag right side out from the 2 ¾" (7 cm)
pening left earlier in the lining. Close the opening with
adder stitch, push the lining inside the bag and press.

5 Top stitch the bag opening 2 mm around
the top edge.

7 Either cut the free ribbon end on the bias or fold it
¼" (0.5 cm) inwards twice and sew.

7 Lay the front and back parts of the bag right sides together and align all edges. Take care to align the identical blocks on the front and on the back.

9 ½" x 11 ¼" (24 x 28,5 cm) D

FRONT SIDE

9 ½" x 11 ¼"
(24 x 28,5 cm)

D

C
9 ½" x 2 ½" (24 x 5,5 cm)

9 ½" x 5 ½" (24 x 14 cm)
B

9 ½" x 7 ½"
(24 x 20 cm)

A

FRONT SIDE

9 ½" x 11 ¼"
(24 x 28,5 cm)

D

C
9 ½" x 2 ½" (24 x 5,5 cm)

9 ½" x 5 ½" (24 x 14 cm)
B

9 ½" x 7 ½"
(24 x 20 cm)

A

BACK SIDE

8 Sew all the way around with a ¼" (0.6 cm) seam allowance while leaving a 2" (5 cm) opening at the shorter side of the D piece for turning.

9 Fold the bottom seam over the side seam so that it forms a triangle and the side seam is centered, measure ¾" (2 cm) from the triangle's peak across the bottom seam and mark it as the middle point. Draw a ¾" (2 cm) line from the middle point both to the right and to the left (total 1 ½" (4 cm)) and sew across this line back-tacking at each end of the stitch line (you can sew

twice across the line to reinforce the stitching). Cut th excess fabric ⅜" (1 cm) away from the seam. Repeat wit the other 3 corners.

10 Turn the bag right side out through the openin and push the lining inside the bag, leaving th button loop outside. Top-stitch around the top of the ba 2 mm from the edge.

11 Sew the wooden button on the front side of th bag approximately 4 ¼" (11 cm) from the bottom.

Reversible Kimono

This reversible kimono was my mother's idea. She said I should definitely have it amongst my book projects as she enjoyed using the ones she made for me and my sister whilst we were babies, and found them very practical..

Don't you think it makes a great gift set with matching mittens for both summer and winter babies?

FINISHED MEASUREMENTS
KIMONO ⊙ 19" x 8 ½" (48 x 22 cm)
MITTENS ⊙ 2 adet 4" x 3 ¼" (10 x 8 cm)

MATERIALS

FOR THE KIMONO

⊕ 23 ½" x 17 ¾" (60 x 45 cm) solid cotton for the outside and the pocket

⊕ 23 ½" x 17 ¾" (60 x 45 cm) floral fabric for the lining and the pocket

⊕ ¾" (1.8 cm) wide, 78 ¾" (200 cm) long, double folded bias tape OR 1 ½" x 78 ¾" (3.6 x 200 cm) fabric to make your own

⊕ 29 ½" (75 cm) long ¼" (0.5 cm) wide velvet ribbon

⊕ Fabric glue

⊕ Thin cardboard or cereal boxes to prepare templates

⊕ DMC 602 (Dark Pink) floss

⊕ Water-erasable or heat-erasable marking pen

FOR THE MITTENS

⊕ 9 ¾" x 9 ¾" (25 x 25 cm) solid cotton

⊕ 9 ¾" x 9 ¾" (25 x 25 cm) floral fabric

⊕ 19 ¾" (50 cm) x ¼" (0.5 mm) suede strip

⊕ DMC 964 (Green) stranded cotton

INSTRUCTIONS

1 Copy the kimono pattern and prepare your templat from thin cardboard.

2 Cut 2 front pieces and 1 back piece from each fabr for both sides of the kimono.

3 Copy the pocket pattern and prepare your templat from thin cardboard. Place the pocket template 1 ¼" (cm) from the right and 3 ¼" (8 cm) from the bottom on th right front piece of the kimono. Trace with a water or hea erasable marking pen around the template.

4 Using a window or light box transfer the teddy be pattern onto the fabric, right above the pocke Embroider the figure with back stitch, using 3 strands o pink stranded cotton.

5 To make the pocket, lay the solid and floral fabric right sides together and put the pocket template o top of them. Trace around with fabric pen and sew on th traced line leaving a 1 ¼" (3 cm) opening at the straigh side of the pocket. Turn the pocket inside out from th gap and press. Top-stitch the straight side of the pocke 2 mm from the edge. Put the pocket to its earlier marke position on the front right side of the kimono and top stitch 2 mm around all edges except the top edge.

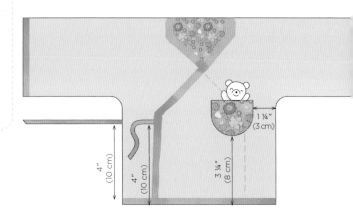

6 Cut the velvet ribbon into three 9 ¾" (25 cm) long equal pieces.

7 For the outside of the kimono with the cotton; align the back piece and two front pieces, right sides together. Place one ribbon piece 4" (10 cm) up from the bottom left side, leaving the raw edge outside. Sew both left and right edges of the kimono and the shoulder.

8 For the kimono lining with the floral fabric; align the back piece and two front pieces, right sides together. Place the second ribbon piece 1 ¼" (3 cm) below the left arm, leaving the raw edge outside. Sew both left and right edges of the kimono and the shoulder.

9 Turn the outside piece right side out. Carefully place the lining into the outside piece. Align and pin all edges.

10 Starting from the neckline sew your store-bought or handmade bias tape all along the front opening and the arm openings. I preferred to machine sew both long edges. Before joining the bias tape to the kimono, I folded it in half lengthways and pressed so that it was easier to sew it around the kimono. You can also use fabric glue to fasten the bias binding in place before sewing.

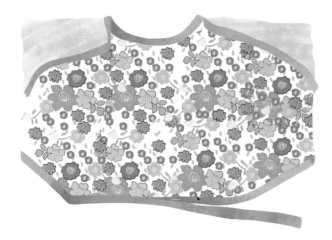

11 Place the third ribbon piece 4" (10 cm) above the bottom edge of the front right while sewing the bias tape leaving it's raw edge inside the seam. Sew bias tape starting and finishing on the neckline so that the joining point shall stay behind the neck.

MITTENS

12 To make one mitten; cut two 4" x 4 ¾" (10 x 1. cm) rectangles from solid cotton and two 4" x ¼" (10 x 11 cm) rectangles from floral fabric. Lay each solid cotton piece against a floral piece, right sides together and sew along the shorter edge. Press seams open.

13 Copy the mitten pattern and prepare you template using thin cardboard. Place you template on the solid cotton and mark the buttonhole position on both the solid and floral sides on one of the joined pieces. Put the buttonhole foot on your sewing machine and make ⅜" (1 cm) long buttonholes.

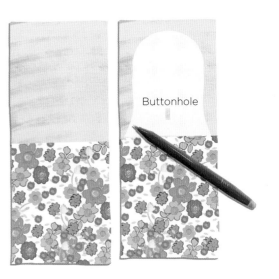

Buttonhole

14 Place the two pieces right sides together. Align the mitten template on the seam and draw around it with an erasable pen. Flip and trace on the opposite part. Sew on the drawn lines leaving a 1 ¼

3 cm) opening on the floral section. Turn the mitten right
de out through this opening.

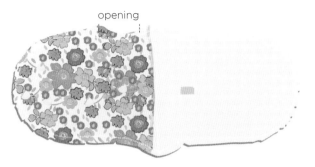

opening

5   Push the lining inside the mitten and press. Using 3 strands of green stranded cotton, sew a running titch all around the buttonhole ¼" (3 mm) away from he buttonhole edges.

6   Cut the suede strip in two and thread it through the buttonholes using a safety pin.

7   Make the second mitten in the same way.

Embroidered Burp Cloth Set & Bag

Burp cloths are essential items if you have a baby. I'm sure that this embroidered burp cloth set in its cute bag would make a great gift for your loved ones with a new-born.

FINISHED MEASUREMENTS
BAG ⊙ 7" x 9 ½" (18 x 24 cm)
BURP CLOTH ⊞ 11" x 11" (28 x 28 cm) each

MATERIALS

FOR ONE BURP CLOTH

⊕ 11" x 11" (28 x 28 cm) white tone-on-tone fabric for the front

⊕ 11" x 11" (28 x 28 cm) solid white cotton for the back

⊕ ¾" (1.9 cm) wide 45 ¼" (115 cm) long double-folded store-bought bias tape or 45 ¼" (115 cm) long 1 ½" (3.8 cm) wide cotton fabric strip to prepare your own

⊕ Water or heat-erasable marking pen

FOR EMBROIDERIES

⊕ DMC Stranded Cotton in:
Green - 704
Light rose - 761
Red - 351
Blue - 3811
Dark blue - 3755
Light green- 964
Yellow – 743

FOR THE BURP CLOTH SET BAG

⊕ 20" x 10 ¼" (51 x 26 cm) white tone-on-tone fabric for the outer

⊕ 20" x 10 ¼" (51 x 26 cm) floral fabric for the lining

⊕ 20" x 10 ¼" (51 x 26 cm) batting

⊕ 20 ½" (52 cm) long ribbon

⊕ 2 ¾" x 10 ¼" (7 x 26 cm) floral fabric (same as the lining)

⊕ 1 ⅜" x 10 ¼" (3.5 x 26 cm) fusible web

⊕ Basting spray

⊕ Fabric glue

⊕ Tassel (optional)

⊕ Leather label (optional)

INSTRUCTIONS

BURP CLOTHS

1 Using a light box or a window transfer the embroider patterns to the corners of the burp cloth fronts.

2 *With green stranded cotton:* Straight stitch the gras around the mushroom using 3 strands.

3 *With red stranded cotton:* Backstitch the mushroon cap using 3 strands, and the circles on it using strand. Backstitch the nose and the mouth of the bunn using 2 strands.

4 *With light pink stranded cotton:* Backstitch th mushroom stalk using 3 strands. Fill the circles on th mushroom cap using 1 strand and satin stitch. Backstitc the teddy bear using 3 strands. Backstitch the mouth an the nose of the lamb with 3 strands, then fill the nose wit satin stitch and 1 strand.

5 *With blue stranded cotton:* Backstitch the tedd bear's clothes, lamb's head & body using 3 strands.

6 *With dark blue stranded cotton floss:* Backstitc the lamb's face, eyes, ears and legs using 3 strands Backstitch the bunny's eyes using 1 strand and make french knot for the iris.

7 *With light green stranded cotton:* Backstitch th bunny using 3 strands.

8 *Yellow stranded cotton:* Backstitch or straight stitch the whiskers, ears and tail of the bunny using 3 strands.

9 Lay the embroidered burp cloth fabric onto th backing fabric, wrong sides together, and sew around all edges with a ¼" (0.5 cm) seam allowance.

10 Sew your handmade or store-bought bias tape around the burp cloths. I glue basted the bias tape around the burp clothes and pressed, then machine sewed both sides together at once.

BURP CLOTH SET BAG

1 Draw a diagonal grid with 1 ¼" (3 cm) spacing on the bag outer with erasable pen. Put the batting under it and fuse them with basting spray to prevent slipping. Quilt the bag outer by sewing along the traced lines.

2 Fold the small piece of floral fabric lengthwise and press. Apply fusible web to the back by pressing with hot iron for 5-10 seconds. Peel off the paper backing, position 1 ⅜" (3.5 cm) above the short edge of the quilted piece from step 1. Press to fuse in place. Cut the ribbon in half and sew a ribbon piece along the top and bottom edges of the strip.

3 Lay the floral lining fabric and the quilted piece right sides together and sew all the way around leaving a 2" (5 cm) opening for turning. Turn right side out and close the opening with ladder stitch.

4 Top-stitch the two short edges with 2 mm seam allowance. Lay the work down, with the lining facing towards you and the ribbon strip positioned at the top. Fold the bottom short edge 6 ¾" (17 cm) upwards, join the folded sides with whip stitch to form the bag so that the short edge with the ribbon will form the flap.

5 To decorate, you can sew a tassel accessory at the center of the flap and a leather label to the bottom left corner of the bag.

Chime Bears

Chime toys are among the best gifts for a newborn. Especially if they are handmade and cute!

While designing these chime bears, I chose to make them colorful to draw baby's attention. They are light, soft and portable, making them perfect for on-the-go entertaining.

FINISHED MEASUREMENTS
7 ¾" x 3 ½" (20 x 9 cm)

MATERIALS

⊕ 2 pieces of 9 ¾" x 6" (25 x 15 cm) cotton fabric

⊕ 4" x 4" (10 x 10 cm) felt sheet

⊕ 4" x 4" (10 x 10 cm) fusible web

⊕ Chime / jingle bell

⊕ Toy-fill

⊕ 1 ½" (4 cm) long cotton tape for the tag

⊕ DMC 310 black floss

⊕ Water or heat-erasable marking pen

⊕ Thin cardboard to prepare a template

⊕ 5 ½" (14 cm) long ribbon with check pattern for the bow tie

⊕ 6" (15 cm) long velvet ribbon for the bow tie strap

⊕ 1 ½" (4 cm) long ribbon for the bow tie centre

INSTRUCTIONS

1 Transfer the bear pattern to cardboard to make a template. Cut out the parts where felt will be used (ears, mouth, tummy) from the template and set them aside for later.

2 Place the template onto one piece of cotton fabric and cut out all the way around, leaving a seam allowance as shown. Repeat with the other piece of cotton fabric.

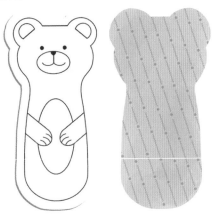

3 Lay the template on the right side of one of the pieces from step 2, and trace inside the cut out sections.

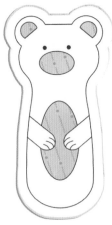

4 Apply fusible web to one side of the felt by pressing with hot iron for 5-10 seconds (note: if using acrylic felt use a protective cloth to prevent the felt from sticking to the iron). Place the cut out template parts on the felt and cut out the ears, mouth, and tummy.

5 Peel off the backing paper and fuse the felt bear parts onto their marked places and sew them to the fabric as close to the edges as possible.

6 With 1 strand of black, backstitch the arms, nose and eyes of the bear and fill with satin stitch where needed.

7 Lay the front and back pieces of the bear right sides together. Put the bear template on the wrong side of the front piece aligning empty areas with felt parts. Draw around the template with an erasable pen (this will be the stitch line).

8 Fold the cotton tape in half aligning its raw edges. Place it between the front and back pieces of the bear 1 ¼" - 1 ½" (3-4 cm) above from the bottom leaving raw edges ½" (0.5 cm) outside the traced line. Pin in place.

9 Sew the front and back pieces all around the traced line leaving a 1 ½" (4 cm) opening on the right side.

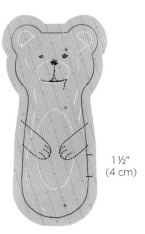

1 ½"
(4 cm)

10 Turn the work right side out and press. Fill with toy-fill or stuffing through the opening, place the chime in the middle. When you consider that the bear is sufficiently stuffed, close the gap with ladder stitch.

11 For the bow tie; align the raw edges of the checked ribbon and sew them with a ¼" (0.5 cm) seam allowance. Sew the small piece of at the center of the checked ribbon puckering to give the bow tie form and placing the seams at the back so as not to show. Wrap the velvet ribbon around the bear's neck joining at the center front and hand sew the bow tie onto the toy, securing both the bow tie and the strap at the same time.

Placemat

I love sewing and gifting placemats.
The ones that I make for babies and
toddlers are my favorites.

You too can make your friends happy
with this simple and cute placemat and
matching coaster.

FINISHED MEASUREMENTS
PLACEMAT ⊙ 12 ¾" x 10 ½" (32,5 x 27 cm)
COASTER ⊙ 3 ½" x 3 ½" (9 x 9 cm)

MATERIALS

FOR THE PLACEMAT

- ⊕ 13 ¼" x 11" (33.5 x 28 cm) fabric for the front

- ⊕ 13 ¼" x 11" (33.5 x 28 cm) fabric for the back

- ⊕ 13 ¼" x 11" (33.5 x 28 cm) batting

- ⊕ 6" x 5 ¾" (33.5 x 15 cm) white lace

- ⊕ 2" (5 cm) long decorative ribbon

- ⊕ DMC 350 red floss

- ⊕ Water or heat-erasable marking pen

FOR ONE COASTER

- ⊕ 4" x 4" (10 x 10 cm) fabric for the front

- ⊕ 4" x 4" (10 x 10 cm) for the back

- ⊕ 4" x 4" (10 x 10 cm) batting

- ⊕ 1 ½" (4 cm) long decorative ribbon

INSTRUCTIONS

1 Copy the "Baby" text (in templates) on to freezer paper and tape it to a sunny window. Tape the bottom right corner of the lace on the writing leaving a 3 ¼" (8.5 cm) distance from the right edge. Transfer the text onto the lace with erasable pen. Backstitch the writing on the lace using 3 strands of red cotton. You can also write the baby's name instead of "Baby" to personalize this item.

2 Lay the front piece of the placemat on the batting and then sew two lines of stitching along the width of the lace, one 1" (2.5 cm) and the other 5" (13 cm) away from the right edge, sewing all three layers. Using 3 strands of red stranded cotton sew 3 wraps of straight stitch on the upper ¾" (1.5 cm) part of both seams.

stitch line

stitch line

Baby

Batting

44

3 Lay the front piece and the back piece of the placemat right sides together. Sew all the way around, leaving a 2" (5 cm) opening for turning. Turn right side out and press. Close the opening with ladder stitch.

4 Fold the ribbon in half. Turning its raw edges under, hand sew one side to the front, and the other to the back of the placemat 1 ¼" (3 cm) below the upper left corner with an applique stitch.

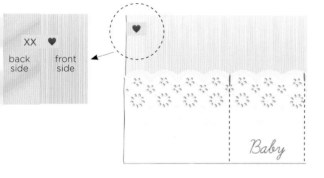

5 To make the coaster; lay front and back pieces right sides together, lay batting on them and sew all the way around leaving a 1 ½" (4 cm) opening. Turn right side out and press. Top stitch around all edges with a ¼" (0.3 cm) seam allowance.

6 Fold the 1 ½" (4 cm) long ribbon in half. Turning its raw edges under, hand sew one side to the front, and the other to the back of the placemat ¾" (2 cm) below the upper left corner with an applique stitch.

Draw-String Fabric Bag

I love fabric bags! They are certainly one of moms' favorite accessories. In a fabric bag, you can put baby's toys, clothes, diapers and anything else you can imagine.

These bags make great gifts too; no one will say no to a cute, fashionable draw-string fabric bag!

FINISHED MEASUREMENTS
12 ¾" x 9 ¾" (32.5 x 25 cm)

MATERIALS

⊕ 2 pieces of 11" x 5 ¼" (28 x 13.5 cm) fabric A (bottom part)

⊕ 2 pieces of 11" x 5 ¾" (28 x 14.5 cm) fabric B (middle part)

⊕ 2 pieces of 11" x 3 ½" (28 x 9 cm) fabric C fabric (upper part)

⊕ 2 pieces of 11" x 13 ¾" (28 x 35 cm) fabric D for the lining

⊕ 3 pieces of 2 ¾" x 2 ¾" (7 x 7 cm) scrap fabric

⊕ One 2 ¾" x 8 ¼" (7 x 21 cm) piece of fusible web

⊕ 23 ½" (60 cm) long cotton lace

⊕ 70 ¾" (180 cm) long cord (draw-string band)

⊕ 2 ½" (6 cm) long ribbon for the tag

⊕ 2 wooden beads

⊕ Circle template made from thin cardboard or cereal box

⊕ DMC Floss

Dark pink - 352
Light pink - 3713
Blue - 794

INSTRUCTIONS

1 Following the instructions under the 'Raw Edge Applique' title in the Techniques section, make 3 circle appliques of 2 ½" (6 cm) diameter from each of the three scrap fabrics and sew them to the middle of one of the fabric A pieces, equidistant as shown in images. I sewed around the appliques as close as possible to the edge using a white thread.

2 Using 3 strands of dark pink stranded cotton, hand stitch a running stitch around the pink circle, 2 mm away from the edge.

3 Using 3 strands of light pink stranded cotton, hand stitch a running stitch around the blue circle, 2 mm away from the edge.

4 Using 3 strands of blue stranded cotton, hand stitch a running stitch around the final circle, 2 mm away from the edge.

5 Aligning the raw edges, sew the cotton lace to one long edge of fabric A.

6 Lay down the right side of one piece of fabric B which will be the middle part of the bag, facing towards you. Place the fabric A piece from the previous step right sides together, on top of it, aligning the lace edge to the other fabric's long edge. Sew along the lace edge. Press the seam towards 'B' and top-stitch on 'B' approximately 2 mm next to the seam.

7 Repeat step 6 to sew a piece of fabric C to B, then fabric D to C. Press the seams between B and C towards B and top-stitch on B, approximately 2 mm next to the seam. Press the seam between C and D open.

8 Prepare the back of the bag in the same way. Sew 4 fabrics (A + B + C + D) to each other right sides together. Do not forget to sew the cotton lace between A and B.

9 Lay down the front and back pieces right sides together aligning all edges. Take care to line up each seam along the sides.

10 Fold the ribbon in half. With raw edges facing outside, center it to the left side of the bag's bottom part and baste in place with a ⅛" (0.3 cm) seam allowance.

11 Sew all edges with a ¼" (0.6 cm) seam allowance as shown in the picture. Leave a 2" (5 cm) opening on the short edge of the lining fabric to turn the bag right side out. In order to pass the cord (or ribbon or any kind of tie), leave a 1 ¼" (3 cm) slit for the casing on both sides of the fabric C.

12 Turn the bag right side out. Close the opening on the lining with ladder stitch. Push the lining inside the bag and top-stitch around the bag opening 2 mm next to the top edge.

13 To form the cord casing, top-stitch around the whole bag along the top and bottom of each side slit so that the lining and the front piece are sewn together all the way around the bag.

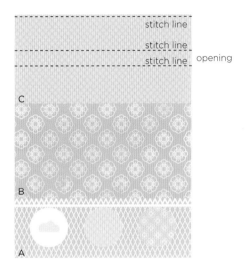

14 Cut the cord into two halves. Using safety pin thread the cord into one of the slits, all the way around through the casing, and out from the same slit. Do the same with the other half of the cord, threading it through the other slit. Thread the wooden beads to the cord ends and make a knot on each.

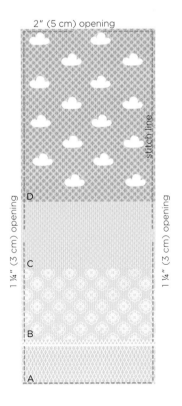

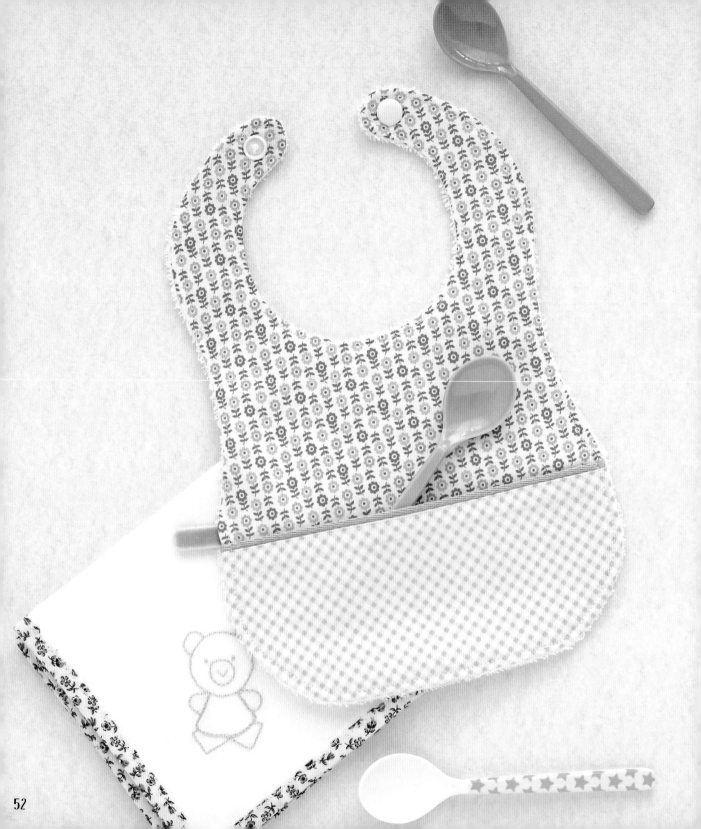

Bib with Pocket

Bibs were one of the first things I learned to sew. To this day, I always include a bib whenever I prepare a gift basket for a new baby.

This simple yet practical bib can be decorated with a cute applique if desired and is suitable both for girls and boys.

FINISHED MEASUREMENTS
11" x 7 ½" (28 x 19 cm)

MATERIALS

FOR THE BIB:

⊕ 12 ½" x 9" (32 x 23 cm) fabric for the front

⊕ 9" x 4 ¼" (23 x 11 cm) fabric for the pocket

⊕ 9" x 4 ¼" (23 x 11 cm) fabric for pocket lining

⊕ 12 ½" x 9" (32 x 23 cm) terrycloth for the back

⊕ 8 ¼" (21 cm) long bias tape

⊕ Plastic snaps

⊕ 2 ½" (6 cm) long ribbon

⊕ Thin cardboard to prepare templates

FOR THE DUCK APPLIQUE;

⊕ 4" x 4" (10 x 10 cm) fusible web

⊕ 4" x 4" (10 x 10 cm) fabric for applique

⊕ 4" (10 cm) long ¼" (0.5 mm) wide ribbon for bow

⊕ DMC 310 black Cotton Perlé No. 8 floss

INSTRUCTIONS

1 Lay the pocket fabric with its right side facing towards you, align one of it's long edges with the long edge of the bias tape and pin. Sew along the edge, with a ⅛" (0.3 cm) allowance. Lay this piece with the lining fabric right sides together, aligning the bias tape attached long edge with one of the lining's long edges, pin and sew along the length with a ¼" (0.6 cm) seam allowance. (bias tape will be sandwiched between the right sides of these two fabrics). Turn right side out and press. Top stitch the pocket front, 2 mm below the bias tape seam.

2 If you would like to add a duck applique to the bib apply fusible web to the back of the applique fabric by pressing with hot iron for 5-10 seconds.

3 Copy the duck pattern and prepare a template using thin cardboard. Put the template on the paper backing of the fusible web and trace around it. Cut out the duck shape on the traced lines.

4 Copy the bib pattern and prepare a template using thin cardboard.

5 Lay the fabric for the front, right side facing up. Lay the pocket piece that you have prepared on the bib and pin aligning the bottom edges. Peel off the paper backing of the duck applique and fuse it to the right of the bib just above the pocket (as shown in the picture) by pressing with hot iron. Make a french knot with the black floss for the eye of the duck.

6 Lay the bib wrong side up. Center the bib template on it (leaving an equal seam allowance all around and trace around the template.

7 Place the bib and terrycloth right sides together, and pin together in a few places.

8   Fold the ribbon in half. Slip it between the terrycloth and the right side of the bib aligning with the upper left edge of the pocket. Pin with the raw edges of the ribbon sticking out ¼" (0.6 cm) outside the pattern line.

9   Sew the terry towel and the bib all around the pattern line leaving a 2" (5 cm) opening for turning.

10 Trim off the excess fabric with pinking shears, to leave an even seam allowance of ¼" (0.6 cm) all round the bib. If you don't have pinking shears, make notches in the seam allowance to avoid bulky seams when you turn the bib right side out.

11 Turn the work right side out from the opening and top-stitch all the way around 2 mm from the edges.

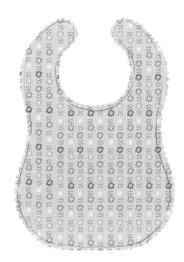

12 Make a bow with the long ribbon and fasten it to the duck's neck by hand.

13 You can use either plastic snaps or velcro strips to fasten the ends of the bib. I used plastic snaps.

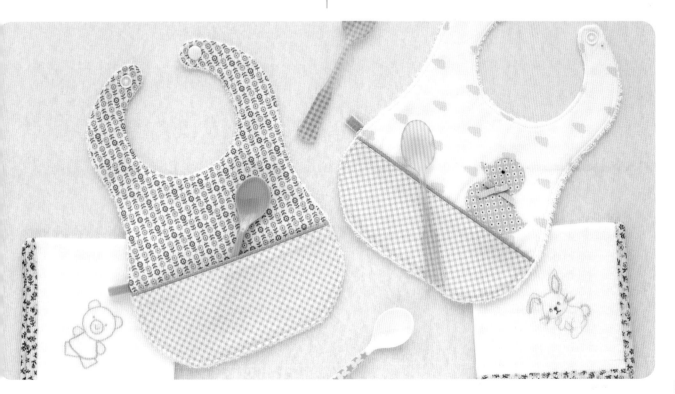

Rabbit Soft Toy

There are few things that makes me as happy as the image of a baby sleeping with a soft toy that I have made.

A sweet, soft, and safe hand made toy is a truly special gift and would be cherished by both mother and baby.

FINISHED MEASUREMENTS
15 ¾" x 4" (40 x 10 cm) including ears

MATERIALS

FOR THE HEAD OF THE RABBIT

⊕ 2 pieces of 4 ¾" x 4 ¼" (12 x 11 cm) linen fabric

FOR THE BODY

⊕ 4" x 4 ¾" (10 x 12 cm) floral fabric

⊕ 2 pieces of 2 ¼" x 4 ¾" (5.5 x 12 cm) floral fabric

FOR THE ARMS

⊕ 4 pieces of 5 ¼" x 1 ⅜" (13.5 x 3.5) linen

FOR THE LEGS

⊕ 4 pieces of 6 ½" x 1 ½" (16.5 x 3.5 cm) linen

FOR THE EARS

⊕ 2 pieces of 3 ¾" x 1 ¾" (10 x 4.5 cm) fabric (ear inner)

⊕ 2 pieces of 4" x 1 ¾" (10 x 4.5 cm) linen (ear outer)

⊕ Toy-fill or stuffing

⊕ 15 ¾" (40 cm) long ribbon

⊕ Thin cardboard to prepare templates

⊕ DMC 310 black Cotton Perlé No. 8

⊕ 2 black safety eyes

⊕ Water or heat erasable marking pen

INSTRUCTIONS

1 Copy the rabbit pattern and prepare templates usin⊕ thin cardboard.

2 Lay the two fabric pieces that will form the back o⊕ the body, right sides together. Sew along the 4 ¾ edge, ¾" (2 cm) at the top and ¾" (2 cm) at the bottom leaving an 3 ¼" (8 cm) opening for turning.

3 Place the piece from step 2 right sides together wit⊕ a linen head piece, short edges centred as show⊕ Stitch across the top edge.

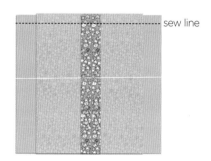

sew line

4 Lay the other linen head piece and the fabric for th⊕ front of the body right sides together centering the⊕ short edges and sew together as in step 3.

5 Draw the nose and mouth of the rabbit on the fabri⊕ with erasable pen, embroider with black floss usin⊕ backstitch for the mouth and satin stitch for the nose.

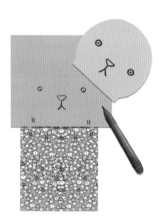

6 Place the inner and outer ear fabrics right sides together. Center the ear template onto them and trace around it. Sew around the pattern line except the straight bottom edge. Turn the work right side out through the unsewn edge and press. Make two.

7 Lay two of the arm pieces right sides together. Center the arm template onto them and trace around it. Sew around the pattern line except the curved edge (you can sew this line twice to reinforce the seams). Turn the right side out through the unsewn edge and press. Repeat with the two remaining arm pieces.

8 Lay two of the leg pieces right sides together. Center the leg template onto them and trace around it. Sew around the pattern line except the straight edge (you can sew this line twice to reinforce the seams). Turn right side out through the unsewn edge and press. Repeat with the two remaining leg pieces.

9 Fill the arms and the legs with toy stuffing. Use a pencil or crochet needle to push stuffing to the ends. Don't stuff all the way up to the up of the arms and legs - leave the top ⅜" (1 cm) empty for sewing onto the body.

10 Lay the back part of the rabbit that you prepared and center the head and the body templates onto it, draw around them. Mark the places for ears, arms and legs while drawing. Put the body parts to their marked places as shown in the picture aligning their raw edges and pin. While placing the ears, fold each ear's bottom ends towards each other at the front so that they meet in the middle. Take care to align the back of the ears with the back of the head. Sew around the pattern lines so that the ears, arms and legs are attached to the back part of the rabbit.

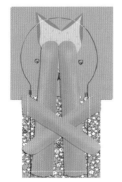

11 Center the head and body templates onto the wrong side of the front part and draw around them. Lay the back and the front of the rabbit right sides together. Fold the body parts towards the body as shown in the picture. Sew the front and the back to each other following the pattern lines leaving an opening for turning. Take care not to sew the body parts while joining the front and the back of the rabbit.

12 Attach the safety eyes to the right places on to the head.

13 Turn the work right side out through the opening. Fill the body and the head with toy stuffing. Close the opening with ladder stitch.

14 Tie the ribbon to the rabbit's neck.

Teething Rings

Your baby is sprouting their first teeth! It may be exciting for parents but it is a real nightmare for your little one. These natural wooden rings will soothe those sore gums and are a safe alternative to the plastic teething toys out there. I'm sure your baby will love them!

FINISHED MEASUREMENTS
Heart ⊕ 5" x 6" (13 x 15 cm)
Star ⊕ 7" x 7" (18 x 18 cm)

MATERIALS

FOR THE HEART

⊕ Five pieces of 1 ½" x 7" (4 x 18 cm) fabrics in assorted designs

⊕ 7" x 6" (18 x 15 cm) cotton fabric for the back

⊕ 7" x 5" (18 x 15 cm) fusible interfacing

⊕ 7" x 5" (18 x 15 cm) oven roasting bag (for the crinkly sound)

⊕ 2 pieces of 6" (15 cm) long, ¾" (1.9 cm) wide bias tape OR 2 pieces of 6" x 1 ½" (15 x 3.8 cm) fabric strips

⊕ 2" (5 cm) long ribbon (optional)

⊕ Thin cardboard to prepare template

⊕ Snaps

⊕ 2 ¾" (6.8 cm) diameter ring made of unfinished wood

FOR THE STAR

⊕ Seven pieces of 1 ½" x 8 ¼" (4 x 21 cm) fabrics in assorted designs

⊕ 8 ¼" x 8 ¼" (21 x 21 cm) cotton fabric for the back

⊕ 8 ¼" x 8 ¼" (21 x 21 cm) fusible interfacing

⊕ 8 ¼" x 8 ¼" (21 x 21 cm) oven roasting bag (for the crinkly sound)

⊕ 2 pieces of 6" (15 cm) long, ¾" (1.9 cm) wide bias tape or 2 pieces of 6" x 1 ½" (15 x 3.8 cm) fabric strips

⊕ 2" (5 cm) long ribbon (optional)

⊕ Thin cardboard to prepare template

⊕ Snaps

⊕ 2 ¾" (6.8 cm) diameter ring made of unfinished wood

INSTRUCTIONS

1 For the heart, sew the five fabric strips t each other; for the star sew seven differer fabric strips to each other along their long edges. Pres seams open and fuse the interfacing to the wrong side c the pieces. Lay the heart and star templates cut from thi cardboard onto the interfacing and trace around them.

2 Put two pieces of ready-to-use bias tapes folde sides together. Fold one of the short edge approximately ⅜" (1 cm) inwards and sew this edge a well as the two long edges to attach the bias tapes t each other. If you are making your own bias tapes; fol the long edges of the fabric strips inwards on the wron side so that they meet in the middle and press, then plac both tapes folded sides together and sew together a before.

3 Fold the ribbon in half aligning its short raw edge: With the raw edges slightly sticking outside th pattern line, place the folded ribbon and prepared bia strips onto the front pieces of the heart and the star an baste in place ⅛" (0.3 cm) from the edge.

4 For the heart; place the front and back pieces righ sides together, with the front fabric on top. Put th oven roasting bag underneath them and sew followin the pattern lines leaving a 2" (5 cm) opening for turning Repeat for the star.

5 Trim off excess fabric with pinking shears, turn th pieces right sides out and top-stitch all around mm from the edges.

6 Fasten snaps to the ends of the bias tapes and attac them to the wooden rings for both heart and sta

TIP: You can wipe the wooden rings to clean. The hea and the star can be washed with baby's clothes.

Rug

Rugs are one of the cutest decorative items for baby's room. For this project, I used assorted sweet fabrics and colorful felts. You can use scrap fabrics from your stash to make this lovely rug for a special little one.

FINISHED MEASUREMENTS
19" x 25 ¼" (48 x 64 cm)

MATERIALS

⊕ 25 ¼" x 19" (64 x 48 cm) linen for the top

⊕ 25 ¼" x 19" (64 x 48 cm) heavy-duty white cotton for backing

⊕ 25 ¼" x 19" (64 x 48 cm) batting

⊕ 16 pieces of 2 ¾" x2 ¾" (7.5 x 7.5 cm) assorted scrap fabrics

⊕ 16 pieces of 3 ¾" x3 ¾" (9.5 x 9.5 cm) assorted wool felt

⊕ 33 ½"x 33 ½"(85 x 85 cm) fusible web

⊕ 1 ¼" (3 cm) wide, 88 ½" (225 cm) long double-folded ready-to-use bias tape OR approximately 88 ½"x 2 ½"(225 x 6 cm) fabric strips to make your own

⊕ Thin cardboard or cereal box to prepare templates

⊕ Basting spray

⊕ 2" (5 cm) long decorative ribbon

⊕ Water or heat erasable marking pen

⊕ Pinking shears

⊕ DMC Stranded Cotton in the following colors:

Dark pink - 893
Light pink - 761
Yellow - 743
Purple - 209
Blue - 775
Dark blue - 813
Light green - 955
Green - 989
Dark green - 3345

INSTRUCTIONS

1 Copy the four circle templates onto thin cardboard and cut out to prepare the templates.

2 Using 2 ¾" (7 cm) diameter circular template for the scrap fabrics and 3 ½" (9 cm) diameter circular template for the felt fabrics, follow "Raw Edge Applique" method explained in the techniques section to make 16 appliques with assorted fabric scraps and 16 felt circles. Cut the perimeter of the felt circles with pinking shears to create a scallop or zig-zag edge.

3 Peel off the backing paper of the fabric appliques and fuse them to the circular felts at the center by pressing with hot iron for 5-10 seconds. Combine appliques and different colored felt pieces as you wish.

4 Place the felt circles with appliques on the 25 ¼" x 19" (64 x 48 cm) linen fabric randomly. After deciding their final places peel off the backing papers and press with hot iron to fuse them onto the linen. Top stitch the appliques 2 mm around their outer edges so that they are well attached to the rug top.

5   Prepare the quilt sandwich; lay the batting, spray the basting on it and place the rug top right side on the wadding, smooth out the wrinkles with your hands and turn the work upside down. Spray baste the other side of the batting and lay the backing fabric onto, smooth out the wrinkles with your hand.

6   For the quilting; draw random circles using 2" (5 cm) and 2 ½" (6 cm) diameter templates on the rug top with erasable pen. Stitch a running stitch on the lines using 3 strands of cotton in assorted colors.

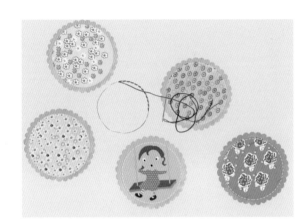

7   To sew bias binding to the rug; you can use store-bought or self-made double folded bias tape to sew round the rug. I sewed one of the long edges of the bias tape to the rug top, and handstitched the other long edge to the backing fabric. While doing so, you can also sew the decorative ribbon folded in half to the rug top, its raw edges will be caught by the bias binding. Please check techniques section under Bias Binding for details.

Pillow with Tents

I love tents for decorating a child's room. While designing this pillow, I was inspired by one of my favorite cartoons when I was a kid. This pillow is both a special and practical gift alternative. It would be great for your own child's room too!

FINISHED MEASUREMENTS
13 ¼" x 17" (34 x 43 cm)

MATERIALS

⊕ 17" x5" (43 x 13 cm) brown checked fabric for the front

⊕ 17" x 8 ¾" (43 x 22.5 cm) cloud fabric for the front

⊕ For the tents (from larger to smaller); 6" x 6 ¾" (15 x 17 cm), 5" x 6" (13 x 15 cm), 4" x 4 ½" (10 x 11.5 cm), 3 ½"x 4 ¼" (9 x 10.5 cm) assorted fabrics

⊕ 2 pieces of 9 ¾" x 17" (25 x 43 cm) cotton fabric for the back

⊕ 3 ¼" x 5" (8 x 13 cm) cloud fabric

⊕ 6" x 21 ½" (15 x 55 cm) fusible web

⊕ 13 ½" x 16 ¾" (34 x 43 cm) batting

⊕ 13 ¼" x 17" (34 x 43 cm) cotton fabric for the lining

⊕ 1 ¼" (3 cm) wide, 62 ¾" (160 cm) long double-folded ready-to-use bias tape OR 62 ¾" x 2 ½" (160 x 6 cm) fabric strip to make your own

⊕ Basting spray

⊕ ¼" (3 mm) wide, 6" (15 cm) long suede strips in 4 different colors

⊕ Thin cardboard or cereal box to prepare templates

⊕ Decorative wooden label (optional)

⊕ DMC Stranded Cotton in the following colors:

Blue - 3766
Dark pink - 760
Dark blue - 519
Light pink - 151

⊕ DMC Cotton Perle Floss No. 8 white

INSTRUCTIONS

1 Sew the brown checked fabric and the cloud fabri right sides together alinging their long edges. Pres seams open.

2 Copy tent patterns and prepare templates usin thin cardboard or cereal boxes.

3 Apply fusible web to the back of the tent and clou fabrics and press with hot iron 5-10 seconds to fuse Place the tent templates on the paper backing of eac piece, trace around, and cut on the traced lines. Repea for the cloud.

4 Cut suede strips into 4 equal pieces.

5 Lay the front piece right side up. Peel off th backing paper on the tent appliques, place them o the pillow front, tuck the suede strips underneath the ti of each tent, and press with hot iron for a few seconds t fuse. Repeat for the cloud. Sew around the appliques a close to the edges as possible.

6 Lay the lining fabric wrong side up, place battin on top of it, and finally the pillow front, right sid up. Fasten these layers to each other with basting spra or pins. Stitch a running stitch around the tents using strands of cotton and the cloud using DMC Cotton Perle Secure the suede strips by making decorative wraps o their joining points to the tent tops.

7 You can handstitch any pattern you like on th tents. I embroidered the first two tents followin their fabric patterns.

8 Fasten the (optional) wooden label to the pillo top on the right side.

9 To finish the back, fold back the long edge of one piece of backing fabric inwards by ¾" (2 cm) and press. Fold the same edge inwards one more time, press, and top stitch next to the edge. Repeat with the second piece of backing fabric.

10 Lay down the pillow front wrong side up, then the back pieces their right sides up on top of it aligning all raw edges and pin. Sew all the way around and turn inside out through the opening at the back.

11 Sew your store-bought or self-made bias tape around the pillow. I machine sewed one edge of the bias tape to the front and fastened the other edge to the back by hand stitching.

Mom's Carry-all Bag

I designed this bag considering the needs of a mother taking her baby out. My priority was to make it big, yet light.This machine washable bag can easily be hung on the stroller's handle or carried on the shoulder. Sew it for a friend or for yourself!

FINISHED MEASUREMENTS
16 ½" x 14 ½" (42 x 37 cm)

MATERIALS

- 17 ½" x 16 ½" (44 x 42 cm) floral linen canvas for the front

- 17 ½" x 16 ½" (44 x 42 cm) solid linen canvas for the back

- 2 pieces of 17 ½" x 16 ½" (44 x 42 cm) cotton fabric for the lining

- 2 pieces of 17 ½" x 16 ½" (44 x 42 cm) medium weight fusible interfacing

- 15 ¼" x 12 ¼" (39 x 31 cm) floral linen canvas for the front pocket

- 15 ¼" x 12 ¼" (39 x 31 cm) cotton fabric for the front pocket's lining

- 12 ¼" x 7" (31 x 18 cm) checked cotton fabric for the front pocket's flap

- 12 ¼" x 7 ¼" (31 x 18 cm) cotton fabric for the lining of the front pocket's flap

- 11 ¾" x 10 ¼" (30 x 26 cm) floral linen canvas for the back pocket

- 11 ¾" x 12 ½" (30 x 32 cm) checked fabric for the back pocket's lining

- 2 pieces of 9 ¾" x 8 ¼" (25 x 21 cm) fabric for the inner pocket

- 9 ¾" (25 cm) long ribbon or cotton tape for the inner pocket

- 4 pieces of 19 ¾" (50 cm) long (i.e. total 78 ¾" (200 cm) long) 1" (2.5 cm) wide cotton webbing for the straps

- 78 ¾" (200 cm) long cord

- 78 ¾" (200 cm) long 1 ¼" (3 cm) wide, diagonally cut checked fabric strips to make bias tape

- 2 wooden buttons

- 2 pieces of 2 ½" (6 cm) long ribbon

- Thin cardboard or cereal boxes to prepare templates

- 1 decorative label (optional)

INSTRUCTIONS

1 Lay the floral and the lining fabric for the fron pocket right sides together, and sew all aroun leaving a 2" (5 cm) opening for turning. Turn right sid out and close the opening with ladder stitch.

2 Lay the checked fabric and lining for the front pocket flap right sides together. Place the flap templat cut out from thin cardboard onto it and trace around th template. Sew following the drawn lines leaving a 2" (cm) opening for turning. Make Trim off excess fabric wit pinking shears, turn the piece right side out, smooth out th seams, close the opening with ladder stitch, and press.

3 Make a buttonhole matching the width of your butto at the center of the flap approximately 1" (2.5 cm) fror the bottom. (You can also use snaps for the fastening an sew a decorative button on the outside)

4 Iron the fusible interfacing to the wrong side of th floral fabric for the front to give it some rigidit Position the flap on the front fabric right sides togethe according to the drawing below [2 ½" (6.5 cm) from lef and right, 11 ½" (29 cm) from the bottom] and sew alon the stitch lines shown.

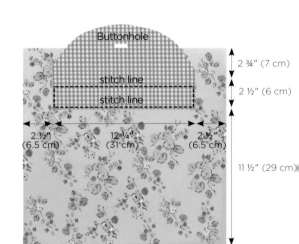

5 Align the long edge of the front pocket with the upper seam line of the sewn flap, fold the right and left sides into pleats like an accordion to obtain a 12 ¼" (31 cm) width. Position the front pocket right side up, 2 ½" (6 cm) from the bottom (as shown in the below drawing), pin and press with hot iron to fix the pleats on the accordion sides. Fold one of the short pieces of ribbons in half, place it on the bottom left edge of the pocket leaving it's raw edges approximately ⅜" (1 cm) inside the pocket and pin. Sew first the accordion sides of the pocket on the left and on the right, back-tacking at the ends to secure the stitching. Then sew the bottom edge in the same manner. If you wish, you can now sew a decorative label to the bottom right corner of the pocket. Sew a button aligning it's position to the buttonhole. The front of the bag is now complete.

around the 3 raw edges. Leave a 2" (5 cm) opening for turning (Step 4). Turn the piece right side out, straighten the edges, close the opening by ladder stitch and press. Top stitch the folded top edge of the pocket (Step 5). Make a buttonhole at the center as wide as your button (you can also use snaps for closure).

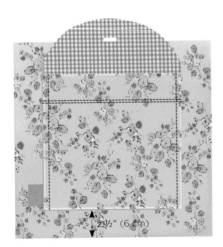

6 Lay the floral and the checked lining fabric for the back pocket right sides together aligning the 11 ¾" (30 cm) edges and sew along this edge (Step 1 in drawing below). Lay down this piece, wrong side of lining facing up, and the seam on top. Fold it backwards 1 ¼" (3 cm) from the top, then press (Step 2). Sew the folded edge to the right side of the pocket (Step 3). Fold the lining again towards the pocket right sides facing each other, align the 3 raw edges and the folded top edge, then sew

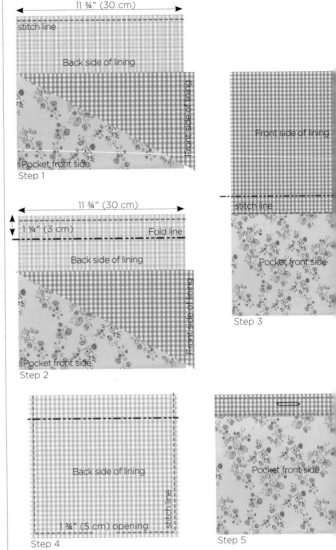

7 Iron the fusible interfacing to the wrong side of the back fabric. Position the back pocket you prepared earlier in the middle, 3 ¼" (8.5 cm) from the top. Fold the second short piece of ribbon in half and place it at the bottom right of the pocket 1" (2.5 cm) from the bottom, leaving its raw edges approximately ½" (1 cm) in the pocket and pin. Sew the right and left edges of the pocket first, then the bottom edge. Sew your wooden button aligning it's position to the buttonhole.

8 Sew the long ribbon along its upper and lower long edges to to the top of the inner pocket fabric, ⅜" (1 cm) below from the top edge. Lay the lining and front pieces of the inner pocket right sides together and align raw edges. Sew all around with a ⅜" (1 cm) seam allowance leaving a 2" (5 cm) opening at the bottom for turning. Turn right side out, straighten the edges and press. Position the inside pocket on the middle of one of the pieces of cotton for the bag's lining, leaving equal distance from right and left, and 4 ¼" (10.5 cm) from the top. Pin and sew and sew around the pocket's three edges.

9 For the straps; cut 1 ¼" (3 cm) wide diagonal strips from the fabric you will use to prepare bias tape, join the strips as explained in the techniques section to make 4 pieces of 19 ¾" (50 cm) bias strips. Fold the bias strips in half lengthwise, wrong sides facing, place the cord in the middle of the strips and sew next to the cord along the length of the fabric to prepare your piping. Align the piping with the long edges of the cotton webbing as shown in the drawing (you can use fabric glue to avoid slipping). Position the other cotton webbing on the back of the first one. Sew both long edges as close to the edge as possible. Make the second strap in the same manner.

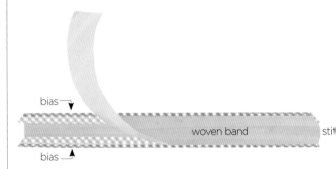

bias

bias

woven band   sti

10 Attaching the straps to the bag; center one o the straps to the front and the other one to th back of the bag at the top edge, leaving a 4 ¾" (12. cm) distance between the straps on each side. Sew each strap to the respective side of the bag right side together, aligining raw edges.

11 Lay the lining piece with inside pocket against th back piece, and the other lining piece against th front piece right sides together and pin. Sew both along the upper edge with a ¾" (1.3 cm) seam allowance. Press seams open. Lay down the two pieces you just made righ sides together, lining against lining, and the back piec against the front piece. Align and pin the central seam together to prevent slipping. Sew around all raw edge leaving a 3 ¼" (8 cm) opening somewhere in the linin the the lining for turning. Before turning right side ou fold all corners of both the lining and the bag in a triangl shape i.e. bottom seam over the side seam and mark a ½" (6 cm) long line. Sew this line twice to reinforce th seams. Turn the bag right side out, close the opening b ladder stitch, push the lining into the bag and press. To stitch all around the top edge.

Peter Pan Collar

I think we all agree on the cuteness of the Peter Pan collar. Doesn't this little touch elevate a simple t-shirt or dress to an absolutely different level?

FINISHED MEASUREMENTS
9 ½" x 5" (24 x 13 cm)

MATERIALS

⊕ 9 ¾" x 6" (23 x 15 cm) linen

⊕ 9 ¾" x 6" (23 x 15 cm) floral

⊕ 9 ¾" x 6" (23 x 15 cm) medium weight fusible interfacing

⊕ 24 ½" (62 cm) long ¼" (0.5 cm) wide suede strips

⊕ Thin cardboard or cereal box to prepare template

INSTRUCTIONS

1 Copy the collar pattern and prepare your template using thin cardboard. Pattern is given for half of the collar therefore fold the cardboard in half and align the straight edge of the pattern with the folded line to prepare your template.

2 Cut the interfacing using the collar template.

3 Lay the linen on a flat surface, and the floral fabric on top of it right sides together. Position the fusible interfacing on top of them and iron it to the wrong side of the floral fabric.

4 Cut the floral and linen fabric all the way around, leaving a ¼" (0.6 cm) seam allowance as shown.

5 Cut the suede strip in half. Fasten both strips to the ends of the collar using fabric glue or pins so that they are sandwiched between the linen and the floral fabrics.

6 Sew around the collar next to the interfacing leaving a 2" (5 cm) opening at the center back for turning (being careful not to catch the suede strips).

7 Before turning make small notches with scissors around the collar to avoid bulk.

8 Turn the collar right side out and press. Close the opening using ladder stitch. Top stitch 2 mm around the edges.

You can also handstitch around the collar using 3 strands of DMC stranded cotton for a cute touch.

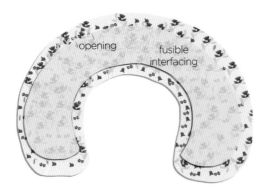

Toy Basket

Baskets are functional to store baby's toys, diapers, caring products or clothes and also add a decorative touch to baby's room.

This basket is soft, machine-washable and a perfect size to let babies grab the handles and drag along.

FINISHED DIMENSIONS
11 ½" x 6 ¾" x 7 ¼" (29 x 17 x 18.5 cm)

MATERIALS

⊕ 25 ¾" x 21 ¼" (66 x 54 cm) linen canvas for bag outer

⊕ 25 ¾" x 21 ¼" (66 x 54 cm) lightweight cotton fabric

⊕ 28 ¼" x 23 ½" (72 x 60 cm) cotton fabric for the lining

⊕ 25 ¾" x 21 ¼" (66 x 54 cm) batting

⊕ 7 ¾" x 7" (20 x 18 cm) cotton fabric for the pocket

⊕ 7 ¾" (20 cm) long ribbon

⊕ Water or heat-erasable marking pen

⊕ Basting spray

⊕ 1 ¼" x 11 ½" (3 x 29 cm) felt strips with ¼" (3-4 mm) thickness for the handles

⊕ DMC Stranded Cotton Floss - Green 912

INSTRUCTIONS

1 On the outer fabric, draw rows of parallel line diagonally in both directions, 1 ½" (4 cm) apar from each other, with an erasable pen. Lay the batting spray baste and lay the outer fabric right side up ont it. Turn them upside down, with the batting now on top spray baste and lay the lightweight cotton fabric ont it smoothing out the wrinkles with your hands. Quilt o the traced lines to make a quilted diamond grid. I used different color thread for more contrast.

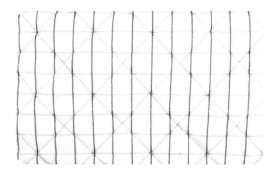

2 Cut out 7" x 7" (18 x 18 cm) squares from each corne of the quilted fabric to create the sides of the basket

3 Fold the pocket fabric in half, right sides togethe Sew around all 3 open edges leaving a 1 ½" (4 cm opening for turning. Turn right side out and press.

4 Sew the ribbon to one of the long edges of th pocket along both ribbon's long edges, folding th raw ends inwards.

5 Lay the basket outer right side up and position th pocket onto it as shown in the drawing. Sew th pocket's 3 edges. If you wish, you can make a vertica seam on the pocket dividing it in half.

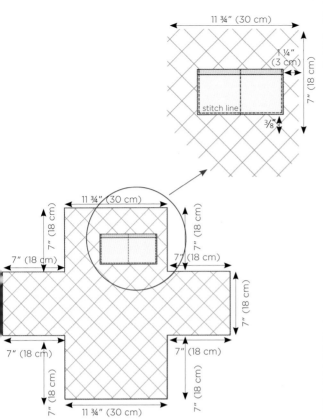

On the wrong side of the basket outer, align the 7"
(18 cm) edges at each of the four corners and sew
them to each other to create the basket shape. Turn the
basket right side out.

sew line

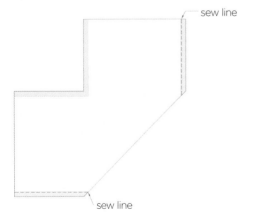

sew line

Cut out 8 ¼" x 8 ¼" (21 x 21 cm) squares at each
corner of the lining fabric. Align these cut edges
s in the previous step, right sides together and sew to

create the basket lining.

8 Place the lining in the basket aligning the seams at
the corners. Fold the surplus of the lining outwards,
fold its raw edges under and pin around the basket. Top
stitch ¼" (2-3 mm) from the folded lining edge all around
the basket.

9 Pin the handles to the shorter sides of the basket
1 ½" (4 cm) from the top and ⅜" (1 cm) from the
corners. Make a cross using 6 strands of DMC stranded
cotton to fasten the handles to the basket.

TIP As the batting may slip while quilting, you may
consider cutting it slightly bigger and cut the excess
edges after quilting.

Cute Fabric Boxes

Fabric boxes are objects that I use the most at home. Sew them for your baby's room or as a gift for your friends.

FINISHED MEASUREMENTS
Small size boxes with checked fabric ⊕ 3 ½" x 3 ½" x 2 ½" (9 x 9 x 6) cm), make 4
Tray ⊕ 7 ¾" x 7 ¾" (20 x 20 cm)

MATERIALS

FOR THE BOXES

⊞ 4 pieces of 8 ¼" x 8 ¼" (21 x 21 cm) checked fabric in different colors

⊞ 4 pieces of 8 ¼" x 8 ¼" (21 x 21 cm) white cotton for the lining

⊞ 4 pieces of 8 ¼" x 8 ¼" (21 x 21 cm) medium weight fusible interfacing

⊞ 4 pieces of 15 ¾" (40 cm) long 1 ¼" (3 cm) wide ready-to-use double-folded bias tape in different colors OR 4 different fabric strips each measuring 15 ¾" (40 cm) long,2 ½" (6 cm) wide to make your own.

FOR THE TRAY

⊞ 2 pieces of 9 ¾" x 9 ¾" (25 x 25 cm) cotton fabric

⊞ 9 ¾" x 9 ¾" (25 x 25 cm) medium weight fusible interfacing

⊕ DMC Stranded Cotton in the following colors:

Yellow - 726
Green - 912
Pink - 892
Light pink - 3713

INSTRUCTIONS

FOR THE BOXES

1 Measure and cut out 2 ¼" x 2 ¼" (5.5 x 5.5 cm) square from each corner of the checked and white fabrics

2 Cut out 2 ½" x 2 ½" (6 x 6 cm) squares from each corne of the 8 ¼" x 8 ¼" (21 x 21 cm) fusible interfacing.

3 Lay the checked fabric wrong side up, center the fusible interfacing onto it and press with hot iron to fuse.

4 Fold the box outer in half diagonally as shown in the drawing and sew two open edges from the borde of the interfacing edge. Push the centre open and fold the box in the other direction, and sew the other two open edges to create a box, turn upside down. Press seam: open and turn right side out.

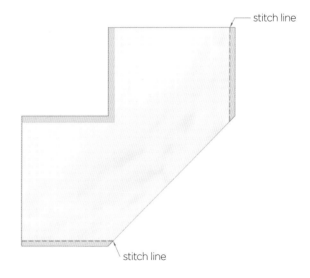

stitch line

stitch line

5 In the same manner, fold the lining fabric in half diagonally, sew two edges. Fold it then on the opposite side to sew the other two edges, press seams open.

6 Place the lining in the box aligning the corners.

7 Press the box to fix the fabrics in place.

8 Sew your store-bought or self-made bias tape around the top edge of the box. To do so, fold the bias tape lengthwise and press, cover the top edge all around with the folded bias tape and pin. Sew all around the edge, catching both sides of the bias tape and enclosing raw edges.

9 Repeat the same steps for the other three boxes.

FOR THE TRAY

10 Lay the outer fabric wrong side up, center the fusible interfacing onto it and press with hot iron to fuse. Turn the piece upside down, place the inner fabric on top, wrong side facing up. Sew all the way around leaving a 1 ½" (4 cm) opening.

11 Turn the tray right side out, sew all 4 edges approximately ¼" (3 mm) around the edges. Then top-stitch again ¾" (2 cm) all the way around.

12 Fold the corners of the tray to form small triangles with the adjacent edges, fasten each corner by hand stitching with 4 strands of DMC stranded cotton ¾" (2 cm) from the edge.

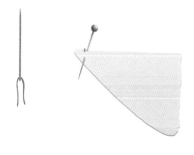

Tiny Bow Ties

Who can not resist bow ties like me? Bow ties always make me smile wherever and for whatever reason they are used. You can sew them to decorate a simple baby overall, a hair clip or gift packages.

FINISHED MEASUREMENTS
2 ¾" x 1 ½" (7.2 x 3.8 cm)

MATERIALS

⊕ 6 ¼" x 3 ¼" (16 x 8 cm) cotton fabric

⊕ 1 ½" x 2" (4 x 5 cm) cotton fabric

⊕ Hair clip or brooch pin

INSTRUCTIONS

1 Fold the large fabric in half, wrong sides togethe
aligning its two long edges. Sew together to create
a tube. Turn inside out, fold the two open edges over so
they meet in the middle, and press.

2 Align raw edges of two short sides and sew
Turn the piece so the seam is hidden.

3 In the same manner, fold the small fabric aligning
it's long edges and sew together to create a tube
Turn the right side out and press, positioning the seam a
the center back.

4 Pucker the bigger piece at the center giving it a
accordion-like shape, wrap the smaller piece around
it and join its ends at the back with applique stitch.

5 You can sew a hair clip or brooch pin to the back o
your bow tie.

Comets

You are invited to a baby shower and have very little time to prepare a gift. Well, these comets are beautiful, simple, yet elegant accessories. You can sew two comets in less than half an hour and gift them in a cute box.

FINISHED MEASUREMENTS
8 ½" x 8 ½" (22 x 22 cm)

MATERIALS

⊕ 9 ¾" x 9 ¾" (25 x 25 cm) square fabric for the front

⊕ 9 ¾" x 9 ¾" (25 x 25 cm) square fabric for the back

⊕ 9 ¾" (25 cm) long (3 mm) wide colorful suede strips for the tassel. You can also use colorful yarns or ribbons.

⊕ Toy-fill or stuffing

⊕ Thin cardboard or cereal box to prepare template

⊕ Water or heat-erasable pen

INSTRUCTIONS

1 Lay the square fabric for the back right side down, an and place the square fabric for the front on top of right side up, align all edges.

2 Prepare a template using the star pattern.

3 Position the star template on the front piece of th star and trace around it.

4 Place the colorful strips between the two fabrics c one of the intersecting edges of the star and pi In the same manner place the hanging ribbon folded half on the exact opposite corner of the intersecting edg you placed the tassel.

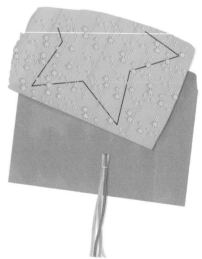

5 Sew all around the traced lines leaving a 1 ¼" (3 cm opening for filling.

6 Fill the star with toy-fill or stuffing being careful t reach all corners, then close the opening by hand o machine.

7 Trim off excess fabric with pinking shears ⅜" (1 cm away from the seams.

Happy Bunny

Among all crafts, embroidery is the one that relaxes me the most; watching the pattern taking form, the freedom of choosing the colors and the stitches, completing a project in a short space of time, and of course the overall cuteness!

This project would be a great welcome gift for a new-born family member.

FINISHED MEASUREMENTS
9 ¾" (25 cm)

MATERIALS

⊕ 11 ¾" (30 cm) diameter cotton fabric or linen

⊕ 2 pieces of 9" x 9" (23 x 23 cm) felt sheet

⊕ 9" (23 cm) diameter embroidery hoop

⊕ 1 ½" x 1 ½" (4 x 4 cm) floral fabric for bunny's dress

⊕ 1" x 1" (2.5 x 2.5 cm) scrap fabric for bunny's ears

⊕ 2 ½" x 2 ½" (6 x 6 cm) fusible web

⊕ Water or heat-erasable pen

⊕ DMC stranded cotton in the following colors:

Black - 310
Green - 563
Light pink - 3713
Dark pink - 760
Red - 350
Light blue - 3811
Dark blue - 3755
Dark green - 3851
Yellow - 743
Orange - 722
Brown - 400
Light brown - 356
Dark brown - 801
Purple - 209

INSTRUCTIONS

1 Using a window or a light box transfer the embroider pattern onto the fabric.

2 *In green:* Backstitch the "Hello Sweet Baby" text using strands and straight stitch the grass using 2 strands.

3 *In red:* Using 2 strands; fill the mushroom caps excep the dots with satin stitch, backstitch the borders c the mushroom. Backstitch the scalloped bottom edge c rabbit's dress with 1 strand.

4 *In light brown:* Backstitch the mushroom stalks an hedgehog's body with 1 strand.

5 *In brown:* Using 2 strands; embroider the stalks of fou flowers with stem stitch; backstitch the hedgehog' face and make a french knot for his nose.

6 *In dark blue:* Using 2 strands; backstitch the border of the butterfly and fill his body with satin stitch backstitch the petals of the flower at the bottom right c the butterfly.

7 *In dark green:* Using 1 strand; backstitch the stalks c five flowers and satin stitch all flower leaves, make french knot in the middle of the pink flower on the right.

8 *In light blue:* Using 2 strands; embroider the cente of the flower near the mushrooms with herringbon stitch, fill the center of the flower near the rabbit with sati stitch, make a french knot for the center of the yellow flower under the mushroom.

9 *In orange:* Embroider the daisy on the right of th rabbit with 3 strands and lazy daisy stitch.

10 *In purple:* Embroider the flower at the bottom and th flower in front of the hedgehog with french knots.

Hello Sweet Baby

Welcome
Baby

1 *In yellow:* Embroider the flower under the mushroom with 2 strands and satin stitch.

2 *In light pink:* Using 2 strands; fill the inside of the flower in rabbit's hand and the petals of the flower in the right of the hedgehog with satin stitch, backstitch the petals of the flower on the left of the rabbit.

3 *In dark pink:* Using 3 strands backstitch the petals of the flower in the rabbit's hand, make a french knot for the center of the same flower, embroider the circle around the pattern with running stitch, embroider an overlapping plus and cross in straight stitches for the petals of the flower at the bottom left of the rabbit.

4 *In dark brown:* Using one strand; backstitch the eyes, nose and mouth of the rabbit and the bird in the mushroom..

5 Prepare templates for the rabbit's ears and her dress. Apply fusible web to the back of the pieces of fabric for the ears and the dress. Place the templates on the paper backing of each and trace around, cut on the traced lines. Peel off the backing paper and fuse the ear and dress appliques in place with a hot iron. Sew round the ears in yellow thread and around the dress in black thread, as close to the edge as you can.

6 *In black:* Using one strand, backstitch the rabbit and the pocket on her dress.

7 Put the inner circle of the embroidery hoop on the felt sheet and draw around inside of it, then cut it out on the traced lines.

8 Put the outer circle of the embroidery hoop on the other felt sheet and draw around inside of it, then cut it out on the traced lines.

9 Once the embroidery is completed, place the small felt circle inside. Run a gathering stitch round the edges on the back of the embroidery as shown, pull the ends of the thread to pucker the edges as much as possible.

Cover the back of the hoop with the larger felt piece and hand sew in place.

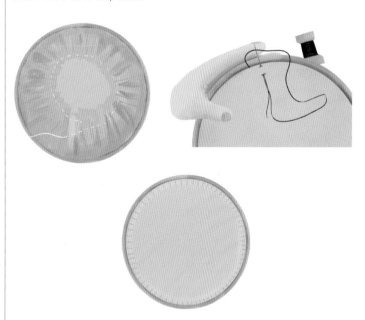

20 You can decorate the screw on the embroidery hoop with a ribbon.

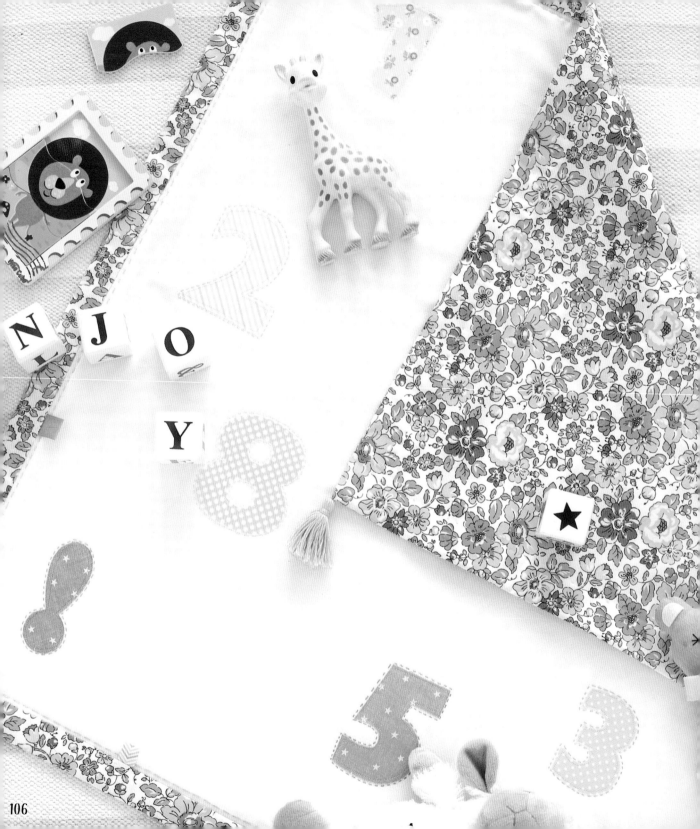

Playmat with Numbers

I designed this soft and plush velvet playmat for babies to happily play on. While creating a clean and soft playing environment you can also help them have fun with the colorful numbers in different sizes.

FINISHED MEASUREMENTS
31 ¾" x 31 ¾" (81 x 81 cm)

MATERIALS

⊕ 31 ¾" x 31 ¾" (81 x 81 cm) white thin velvet fabric for the top

⊕ 36 ½" x 36 ½" (93 x 93 cm) floral fabric for backing

⊕ 31 ¾" x 31 ¾" (81 x 81 cm) batting

⊕ 11 pieces of 4 ¾" x 4 ¾" (12 x 12 cm) assorted scrap fabrics for the numbers

⊕ Approximately 15 ¾" x 15 ¾" (40 x 40 cm) fusible web

⊕ 4 pieces of 2 ½" (6 cm) assorted ribbons

⊕ Basting spray

⊕ Thin cardboard to prepare templates

⊕ DMC stranded cotton in the following colors:

Pink - 3708
Coral - 967
Dark pink - 893
Light pink - 761
Yellow - 743
Cyan - 964
Green - 954
Dark green - 958

INSTRUCTIONS

1 Copy the number patterns and prepare template using thin cardboard.

2 Apply the fusible web to the back of the assorted scrap fabrics by pressing with hot iron for 5-10 seconds.

3 Draw around the number templates on the paper backing and cut out the pieces on the traced lines.

4 Randomly scatter the numbers around the white velvet top.

5 Once you are happy with their positions, peel off the paper backing and fuse the number applique to the velvet by pressing with hot iron for 5-10 seconds (important: use a protective cloth between the iron and the velvet so it doesn't melt and stick to the iron).

6 Sew around the edges of the appliques.

7 Lay down the batting, spray baste and place the velvet on top, right side up. Smooth surface to remove wrinkles.

8 Sew a running stitch around the appliques using strands of stranded cotton as follows: yellow for the numbers 1, 4 and 8; light pink for 6; green for 2 and 3; dark green for 7 and exclamation; dark pink for 0 and 5.

9 Lay the floral fabric for the backing wrong side up, spray with basting spray, lay the placemat (with batting) on top, right side facing up. Smooth out any wrinkles.

10 Fold the surplus edges of the backing fabric towards the placemat top from all 4 sides by 1" (3 cm) twice and press. Fold 4 ribbons in half, place them anywhere on the sides of the placemat hiding their raw edges under the folded edges.

11 Prepare tassels using yellow, green, pink and coral stranded cotton (see the Techniques section for information on how to make tassels). Fasten them to the corners, hiding their raw ends in the folded edges.

12 Attach the folded edges of the backing fabric to the placemat top by hand sewing with applique stitch. Using 3 strands of cyan stranded cotton, sew a running stitch all around the mat approximately 3 mm from the folded edges.

Changing Mat with Cat Pillow

I think this set is one of my favorite projects. A changing mat is one of the most essential items for a mother when out and about.

The cat pillow can be used as a head support when changing diapers or as a toy for your baby.

FINISHED MEASUREMENTS
Cat pillow (ears and legs included) ⊕ 15 ¾" x 8 ¼" (40 x 21 cm)
Changing mat ⊕ 26 ½" x 19" (67 x 48 cm)

MATERIALS

CAT PILLOW

⊕ 7 ½" x 9" (19.4 x 22.6) dot fabric for the front

⊕ 6 ¼" x 9" (16 x 22.6 cm) plaid fabric for the front

⊕ 13 ¼" x 9" (33.8 x 22.6 cm) dot fabric for the back

⊕ 4 pieces of 2 ¾" x 2 ¾" (7 x 7 cm) dot fabric for the ears

⊕ 2 pieces of 1 ¾" x 1 ¾" (4.5 x 4.5 cm) brown fabric for the inside of the ears

⊕ 2 pieces of 1 ¾" x 1 ¾" (4.5 x 4.5 cm) fusible web for the ears

⊕ 2 pieces of 1 ¾" x 3 ¼" (4.7 x 8.5 cm) dot fabric for the arms

⊕ 2 pieces of 1 ¾" x 3 ¼" (4.7 x 8.5 cm) fusible web for the arms

⊕ 2 pieces of 2 ½" x 2 ¼" (6 x 6.5 cm) dot fabric for the feet

⊕ 4 pieces of 2 ½" x 2 ¼" (6.5 x 6 cm) checked fabric for the pockets

⊕ 2 pieces of 2 ¾" (7 cm) long ribbon for the pockets

⊕ 2 ½" (6 cm) long ribbon for the tag

⊕ 2 small buttons

⊕ 1" x 2" (2.5 x 5 cm) felt piece and fusible web for the label at the back

⊕ 1 ½" (4 cm) long cotton tape for the label

⊕ Toy-fill or cotton stuffing to fill the pillow

⊕ Thin cardboard or cereal boxes to prepare templates

⊕ DMC 310 Cotton Perle floss in black

⊕ DMC 3031 stranded cotton in brown

CHANGİNG MAT

⊕ 19 ¾" x 27 ½" (50 x 70 cm) plaid fabric for the mat outer

⊕ 19 ¾" x 27 ½" (50 x 70 cm) dot fabric for the mat inner

⊕ 19 ¾" x 27 ½" (50 x 70 cm) lightweight cotton fabric

⊕ 19 ¾" x 27 ½" (50 x 70 cm) batting

⊕ 6" x 1 ½" (15 x 4 cm) cotton strip for the button loop

⊕ 6" x 6" (15 x 15 cm) plaid fabric for the pocket

⊕ 6" x 7 ¾" (15 x 20 cm) yellow fabric for the pocket

⊕ 6" (15 cm) long ribbon for the pocket

⊕ Button

⊕ 2 ½" (6 cm) long ribbon

⊕ Basting spray

INSTRUCTIONS

FOR THE CAT PILLOW

1 Copy the cat pattern and prepare your templates using thin cardboard.

2 Apply fusible web to the back of the fabrics to be used for the inside of the ears, pressing with hot iron on for 5-10 seconds. Using the template, cut out the triangles for the inside of the ears.

3 Position your inner ear template on the right side of two of the dot fabrics for the ears and trace around , fuse the triangles to their places on the fabric and sew round the appliques next to the edges.

4 Lay the front and back fabrics for the ears right sides together, draw ear pattern on one of them using template and sew on the traced lines leaving the bottom edge open. Trim off excess fabric, turn the ears right side out and press.

5 Using arm pattern, cut 2 arms from the fabric, fold all edges except the curved one ¼" (0,5 cm) inwards. Cut two fusible web pieces (as per arm template but without seam allowance) and fuse these to the wrong side of the arms.

6 Draw pocket pattern using the template on the wrong side of two of the checked fabrics. Place each piece right sides together with another piece of checked fabric (unmarked), and sew on the traced lines leaving a 1 ¼" (3 cm) opening in the middle of the upper straight edge for turning. Trim off excess fabric, turn right side out and press. Align the 2 ¾" (7 cm) long ribbon with the upper straight edge of the pocket, fold ribbon's raw ends under and sew it to the pocket along both long edges. Repeat for the other pocket.

7 Lay the two dotted fabrics for the feet right sides together. Draw the foot pattern on the wrong side of one and sew on the traced lines leaving the straight edge open. Turn the right side out and press. Make two.

8 To embroider the cat's face, copy the pattern onto the dot fabric using a window or lightbox. Backstitch the face features using black cotton perle, fill the center of the nose with satin stitch.

9 Lay the fabrics for the upper and lower pieces of the front right sides together and sew together. Press the seams towards the lower piece. Top-stitch approximately 2 mm below the seam on the lower piece.

10 Press the front of the cat you prepared and lay it right side up. Position the cat template aligning the pattern with the seam and the cat's face, trace around the template. Mark the places of ears, feet, arms and pockets on the front piece using erasable pen. Position the features that you prepared earlier to their respective places on the front piece as shown in the picture.

11 Put the ears on the front piece right sides together and sew in place.

12 In the same manner put the feet in place and sew.

13 Peel off the backing paper on the arms and press with hot iron for 5-10 seconds to fuse in place. Sew 2 mm around the edges.

14 Attach the pockets on the front piece either by hand or machine as seen in the picture. I hand sewed the pockets with running stitch using 2 strands of brown stranded cotton.

15 Fold the 2 ½" (6 cm) ribbon in half. Align it's raw edges with the left edge of the cat and sew.

16 Sew 2 small buttons to their marked places.

17 For the label at the back; cut the felt piece using the template, center and sew the cotton tape onto . Position the label on the right side of the fabric for the back; 2" (5 cm) above the short edge and 1" (2.5 cm) to the right from the long edge. Peel off the backing paper and fuse in place, then sew 2 mm around the edges.

18 Lay the front and back pieces of the cat pillow right sides together aligning all edges and sew all around leaving a 1 ½" (4 cm) opening between the feet for turning. Trim off excess fabric, turn right side out, press, and fill the pillow with stuffing. Close the opening with ladder stitch.

FOR THE CHANGING MAT

19 On the outer fabric, draw rows of parallel lines diagonally in opposite directions, 1 ¼" (3 cm) apart. Lay batting under the outer fabric and the lightweight cotton fabric under the batting. Attach all three layers (outer, batting, lightweight cotton) to each other using basting spray and sew along the drawn diagonal lines in both directions to have a diamond grid quilt. As I was using checked fabric, I used the diagonal lines on the fabric pattern.

20 For the button loop, fold your fabric in ha lengthways, press and open. Fold both lon edges of the fabric inwards meeting at the crease, fol the piece in half again lengthways and press, enclosin all raw edges. Sew the long edges to each other 2 mm from the edge.

21 Lay the two fabrics for the pocket right side together aligning their 6" (15 cm) edges and se together. Press seam open. Sew the ribbon right on th seam joining the two fabrics on the right side, along bot it's long edges.

22 Fold the pocket piece you prepared in half wit wrong sides facing. Sew around the 3 ope edges leaving a 1 ½" (4 cm) opening in the middle of th short edge for turning. Turn right side out and press.

23 Copy the changing mat pattern and prepar your template using thin cardboard.

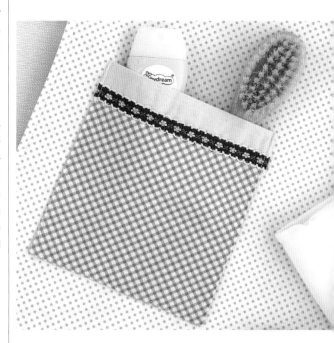

24 Lay the dot fabric for the mat inner right side up, place your template on it and trace around the edges. Position the pocket on the left bottom corner, 2 ¾" (7 cm) above from the bottom and 1 ¾" (4.5 cm) away from the left edge. Sew the pocket to the mat inner 2 mm away all around the three edges.

25 Fold the button loop you prepared in half, align it's raw edges to the upper edge of the mat inner at the center and sew in place.

26 Fold the 2 ½" (6 cm) long ribbon in half and leaving its raw edges in the seam allowance sew it to the mat inner approximately 4 ¾" - 5 ½" (12-13 cm) above from the bottom on the right.

27 Lay the mat outer and mat inner right sides together aligning all edges. Place the mat template on top and trace around it, then sew on the traced lines leaving 2 ½" (6 cm) opening for turning. Turn the right side out and press.

28 Top-stitch all around the mat 3 mm from the edges.

29 Sew the button 12 ¼" (31 cm) above from the bottom on the outer side of the mat.

House Wall Organizer

I had a lot of fun sewing these cute little houses that will bring color to your baby's room. They may take a little bit longer to make than some of the other projects in the book but they are absolutely worth the time you will spend on them. You can use a wood dowel or a clothes hanger to hang them on the wall.

FINISHED MEASUREMENTS
11 ¾" x 10 ¼" (30 x 26 cm)

MATERIALS

⊕ 9 ¾" x 7 ¾" (25 x 20 cm) cotton fabric for the house walls

⊕ 12 ½" x 11 ½" (32 x 29 cm) cotton fabric for the backing

⊕ 12 ½" x 11 ½" (32 x 29 cm) batting

⊕ 12 ½"x 2" (32 x 5 cm) cotton fabric for the roof lining

⊕ 30 pieces of 2 ¾" x 2 ¾" (7 x 7 cm) assorted fabrics for the roof

⊕ 2 pieces of 9 ¾" x 7 ½" (25 x 19 cm) cotton fabric for the pocket

⊕ 9 ¾" x 7 ½" (25 x 19 cm) batting for the pocket

⊕ 4 ¾" x ¼" (12 x 8.5 cm) cotton fabric for the door

⊕ 2 ½" x 2 ¼" (6 x 5.5 cm) cotton fabric for the window

⊕ 26 ¾" (68 cm) long, ¾" (1.8 cm) wide double-folded ready-to-use bias tape OR 26 ¾" x 1 ½"(68 x 4 cm) cotton strip to make your own

⊕ 4" x 7 ¾" (10 x 20 cm) lightweight interfacing for the door and window appliques

⊕ 2 buttons

⊕ Thin cardboard or cereal boxes to prepare templates

⊕ Fabric glue

⊕ Liquid fabric adhesive

FOR THE BLUE HOUSE

⊕ DMC Stranded Cotton in the following colors:

Pink - 352
Blue - 3755
Green - 563

⊕ 3 buttons

FOR THE PINK HOUSE

⊕ 2"x 2½" (5 x 6 cm) felt piece and a slightly larger piece of fusible web

⊕ 1 store-bought mini pompom

⊕ DMC Stranded Cotton in the following colors:

Pink - 352
Dark turquoise - 3851
Green - 563

⊕ 3 buttons

INSTRUCTIONS

1 Prepare the clamshell pieces that will form the roof according to the instructions in the Techniques section. Fold the roof lining fabric in half lengthways and make a crease. Open the fabric and start joining the clamshell appliques aligning their bottom edges to the crease. Continue attaching more clamshells, following the method in the Techniques section.

2 Once the roof is completed, press the piece. Trim ¾" (1.5 cm) along the bottom of the roof lining fabric so that there remains only a ⅜" (1 cm) seam allowance.

3 Align the center of the long edge of the house wall fabric fabric with the center of the 12 ½" (32 cm) long edge of the clamshell roof piece, lay them right sides together and sew. Press the seams towards the house backing. Top-stitch 2 mm below the seam.

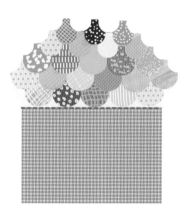

4 Cut the ready-to-use bias tape into two equal pieces. Fold each piece in half lengthways raw edges inside and sew both long edges (If you make your own bias tape, fold the fabric strip in half lengthways to make a crease in the middle, open the fabric and fold the long edges towards the crease then press). You can see the techniques section for preparing a bias tape.

5 Make a buttonhole on one end of each bias tape according to the dimensions of the buttons you will use.

6 Lay the batting, then the house backing fabric for the house right side up on top of it (you can spray baste to fasten these layers). Lay the front piece from step 3 wrong side up on top of them. Place your template on top and trace around it. Place the bias tapes on the top edge of the roof, positioned ¾" (2 cm) on the right and ¾" (2 cm) on the left of each edge, with the tape's raw edges outside. Pin and sew all around the house on the traced lines leaving a 2" (5 cm) opening at the bottom. Trim off excess fabric.

7 Turn the piece right side out press, top-stitch all around 2 mm from the edges.

8 Transfer the grass pattern onto the pocket front using a window or lightbox. Backstitch the grass using 3 strands of green stranded cotton. Sew the buttons in place. For the rabbit on the pink house, apply fusible web to the felt piece. Using rabbit template, draw the pattern on the paper backing of the fusible web and cut out on the traced lines. Peel off the backing paper and fuse the applique to the pocket front. Sew around the rabbit applique, make a cross stitch for the rabbit's eye with pink stranded cotton.

9 Place lightweight interfacing against the right sides of the fabrics for the door and window. Trace the door and window patterns onto the interfacing, and sew on the drawn lines. Make a small, straight cut on the back interfacing using scissors or seam ripper and turn right sides out through this opening. Press.

10 Pin the door and window appliques in place and applique stitch around all their edges to attach. Sew the button on the door as shown in the drawings.

11 Lay down the batting for the pocket, place the fabric for the inside of the pocket right side up aligning all edges. Put the fabric for the outside of the pocket wrong side up on top of them, trace the pocket pattern on and sew on the traced lines leaving a 2" (5 cm) opening for turning. Turn right side out, press and top-stitch all around 2 mm from the edges.

12 Sew a running stitch using 3 strands of pin stranded cotton around the door and blu stranded cotton inside the window. Do the same for th pink organizer, using green stranded cotton around th door and pink inside the window.

13 Sew the mini pompom to the tail of the rabbit o the pink organizer.

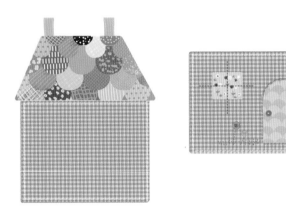

14 Place the pocket on the front of the organize aligning all edges, pin and fasten with whi stitch around three edges leaving the upper edge open

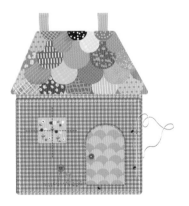

15 Sew the two buttons on the backside of the wa organizer.

Patchwork Blanket

This is one of the projects that I enjoyed
making the most. A patchwork blanket
brings instant joy and color to a room.
You can design your own blanket using
different fabrics & appliques and create a
unique piece to touch a new mother's heart.
It's all up to your imagination!

FINISHED MEASUREMENTS
35 ½" x 35 ½" (90 x 90 cm)

MATERIALS

FOR THE FRONT

- ⊕ 16 pieces of 6" x 6" (15 x 15 cm) assorted fabrics
- ⊕ 4 pieces of 8 ¾" x 8 ¾" (22.1 x 22.1 cm) assorted fabrics
- ⊕ 2 pieces of 28 ¼" x 4" (71.8 x 10 cm) checked fabric
- ⊕ 2 pieces of 35 ½" x 4" (90.2 x 10 cm) checked fabric

FOR THE BACK

- ⊕ 35 ¾" x 35 ¾" (91 x 91 cm) cotton fabric
- ⊕ 35 ¾" x 35 ¾" (91 x 91 cm) batting
- ⊕ 5 pieces of 26 ¾" (68 cm) long decorative ribbon
- ⊕ 2 pieces of 6" x 2 ¾" (15 x 7.5) cm white lace (optional)
- ⊕ 1 ¼" (3 cm) wide, approximately 157 ½" (400 cm) long double-folded ready-to-use bias tape OR 157 ½" x 2 ½" (400 x 6 cm) cotton strip to make your own
- ⊕ DMC Cotton Perle No:8 white
- ⊕ Thin cardboard or cereal boxes to prepare templates

FOR THE HEART

- ⊕ 5" x 5" (13 x 13 cm) floral fabric
- ⊕ 5" x 5" (13 x 13 cm) fusible web
- ⊕ DMC stranded cotton in red - 347

FOR THE CLOVER

- ⊕ 5" x 5" (13 x 13 cm) green fabric
- ⊕ 5" x 5" (13 x 13 cm) fusible web
- ⊕ DMC stranded cotton in green - 704

FOR THE HOUSE

- ⊕ 4 ¼" x 3 ¼" (10.5 x 8 cm) house fabric
- ⊕ 4 ¼" x 1 ¾" (11 x 4.5 cm) roof fabric
- ⊕ 1 ¼" x 1 ¼" (3 x 3 cm) window fabric
- ⊕ 1 ¼" x 1 ½" (3 x 4 cm) door fabric
- ⊕ 2 ½" (6 cm) long ribbon for the chimney
- ⊕ 4 ¾" x 5 ½" (12 x 14 cm) fusible web

FOR THE ELEPHANT & BALLOON

- ⊕ 6 ¼" x 4" (16 x 10 cm) blue fabric
- ⊕ 1 ⅜" x 1 ½" (3.5 x 4 cm) balloon fabric
- ⊕ 6 ¼" x 4" (16 x 10 cm) fusible web
- ⊕ DMC Cotton Perle No:8 black - 310

FOR THE POCKET

- ⊕ 9 ¾" x 6 ¼" (25 x 16 cm) cotton fabric
- ⊕ 6 ¼" (16 cm) long decorative ribbon
- ⊕ 2 ½" (6 cm) long decorative ribbon

INSTRUCTIONS

1 Copy the heart, elephant, balloon, clover and house patterns and prepare a template for each of them using thin cardboard.

2 Apply the fusible web to the wrong sides of the heart, clover, elephant, balloon, house, roof, door and window fabrics pressing with hot iron for 5-10 seconds. Trace around the templates on the back of the fusible web and cut out on the traced lines.

3 Peel off the backing paper on the heart figure and place it at the center of a 6" x 6" (15 x 15 cm) fabric on the right side, pressing with hot iron to fuse in place. Machine sew around its edges. Using blanket stitch, hand sew around the heart applique using 4 strands of red stranded cotton.

4 On a 8 ¾" x 8 ¾" (22.1 x 22.1 cm) fabric, attach the appliques for the house, roof, door and window in the same manner, pressing with hot iron. Before fusing the chimney applique, fold the ribbon to be used here in half and place it's raw ends under the chimney applique on the top. Sew around all edges using brown or black thread.

5 Fuse the clover applique on the other 8 ¾" x 8 ¾" (22.1 x 22.1 cm) fabric piece pressing with hot iron. Sew around its edges. Sew a running stitch around the clover using 4 strands of green stranded cotton floss.

6 Fuse the elephant and balloon appliques on a 8 ¾" x 8 ¾" (22.1 x 22.1 cm) fabric pressing with hot iron and sew around their edges. Using Cotton Perle in black; backstitch the string of the balloon, the elephant's ear and tail, and make the eye and the end of the tail with a french knot.

7 Fold the fabric for the pocket in half along its 9 ¾" (25 cm) edge. Open the fabric, place the ribbon on the right side of the pocket ¾" (1.5 cm) below the crease, sew in place along both it's long edges. Fold the piece in half again but right sides together this time. Sew the pocket around all edges leaving a 1 ½" (4 cm) opening. Turn the right side out and press. Center the pocket on its backing fabric, fold the 2 ¼" (6 cm) ribbon in half and position it at the bottom right of the pocket leaving its raw ends inside the pocket, sew around the three edges leaving the upper edge open.

8 Join two 8 ¾" x 8 ¾" (22.1 x 22.1 cm) fabric pieces you prepared as shown in the picture sewing with a ¼" (0.8 cm) seam allowance and press the seams to the left. Join the other two fabric pieces in the same manner and press the seams to the right. Then join these pieces together, sewing with a ¼" (0.8 cm) seam allowance. You now completed the 4 pieced fabric group at the center (Steps 1, 2 & 3)

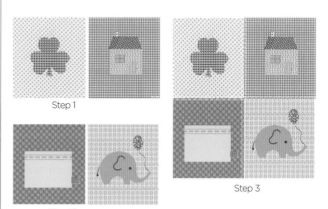

Step 1

Step 2

Step 3

9 Join three 6" x 6" (15 x 15 cm) fabrics sewing with a ¼" (0.8 cm) seam allowance, press seams open, and sew the long edge of the joined fabrics to the left of the 4 pieced group at the center with the same seam allowance. Repeat the same to the right of the center. When joining the pieces, place two of the 2 ¼" (6 cm) ribbons folded in half to the places shown on the pictures (Steps 4, 5, 6 & 7). I added a lace strip on the bottom square of the fabric group on the right for a cute touch.

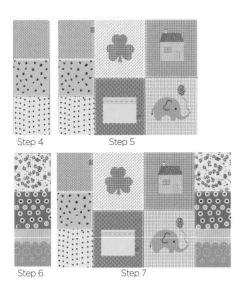

Step 4   Step 5

Step 6   Step 7

10 Join five 6" x 6" (15 x 15 cm) fabrics sewing with a ¼" (0.8 cm) seam allowance, then sew this piece above the quilt centre. Repeat to add a row of 5 blocks to the bottom of the quilt centre. When joining the pieces, place two of the 2 ½" (6 cm) ribbons folded in half to the places shown on the pictures aligning its raw ends (Steps 8, 9, 10 & 11).

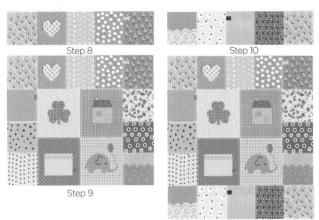

Step 8   Step 10

Step 9

Step 11

11 Sew the two 28 ¼" x 4" (71.8 x 10 cm) checke fabrics to the upper and lower edges of the qui centre with a ¼" (0.8 cm) seam allowance. In the sam manner, sew the two 35 ½" x 4" (90.2 x 10 cm) fabrics t the right and to the left. Press seams open (Step 12 & 13,

Step 12   Step 13

12 Prepare the quilt sandwich. Lay the batting, spra baste, lay the patchwork on top and smooth ou the wrinkles with your hand. Flip over, now the batting on the top, and spray baste. Place the backing fabric o the wadding, right side facing up, smoothing the wrinkle out.

13 Quilt by hand or sewing machine. I quilted b hand using white Cotton Perle. After quilting, trir the excess backing fabric and batting.

14 Sew the bias binding; you can use double-folde store-bought bias tape or make your owr To make your own, join 2 ¼" (6 cm) wide fabric strip to each other until the piece measures 157 ½" (400 cm Fold the strip In half lengthways, use the technique c your choice for bias binding. I sewed one edge of the bia tape to the quilt top on the machine, and fastened th other edge to the backing by hand. For more, you ca check the "bias binding" title in the techniques section.

Templates

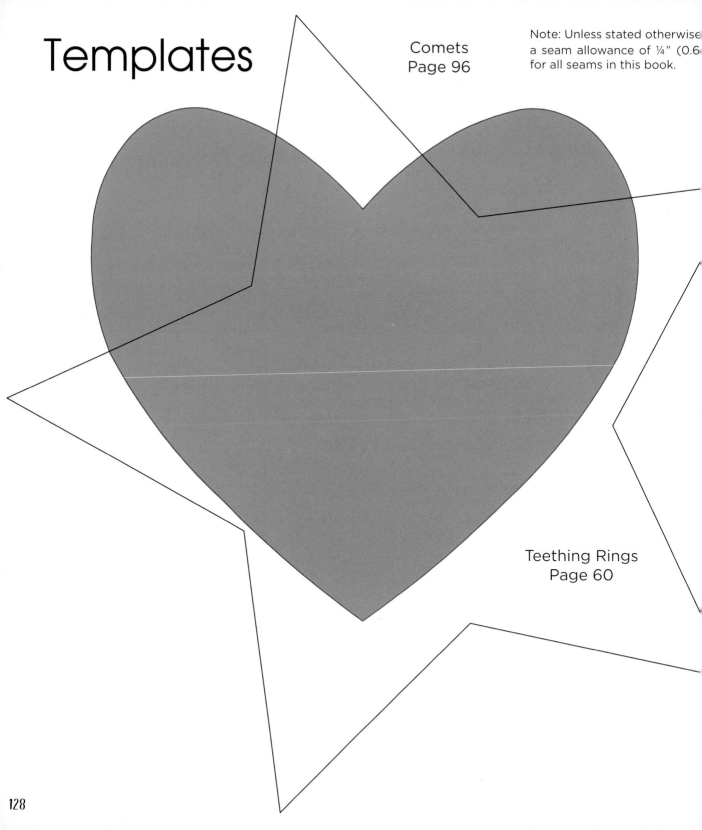

Comets
Page 96

Note: Unless stated otherwise a seam allowance of ¼" (0.6 for all seams in this book.

Teething Rings
Page 60

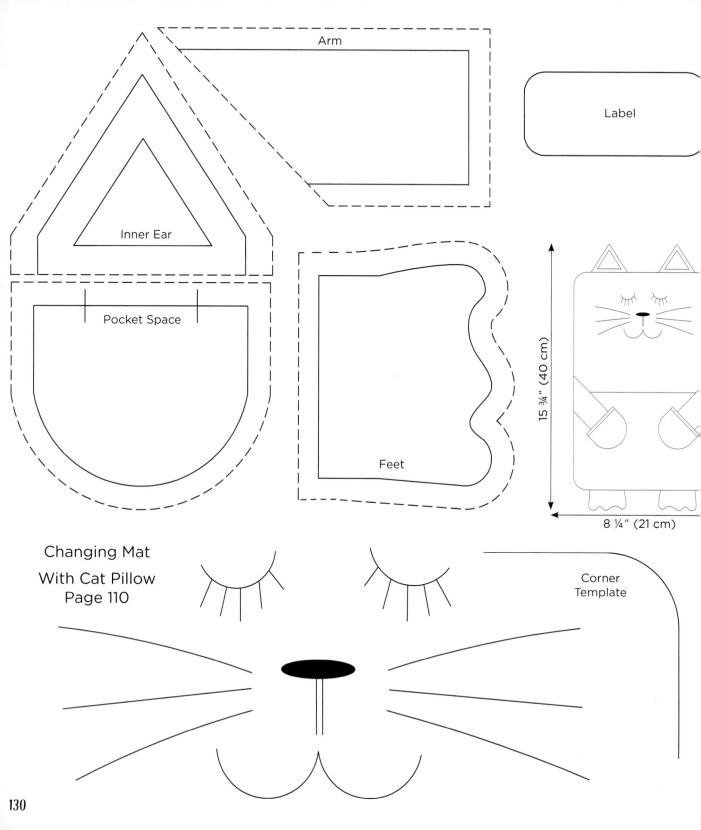

Arm

Label

Inner Ear

Pocket Space

Feet

15 ¾" (40 cm)

8 ¼" (21 cm)

Changing Mat

With Cat Pillow
Page 110

Corner
Template

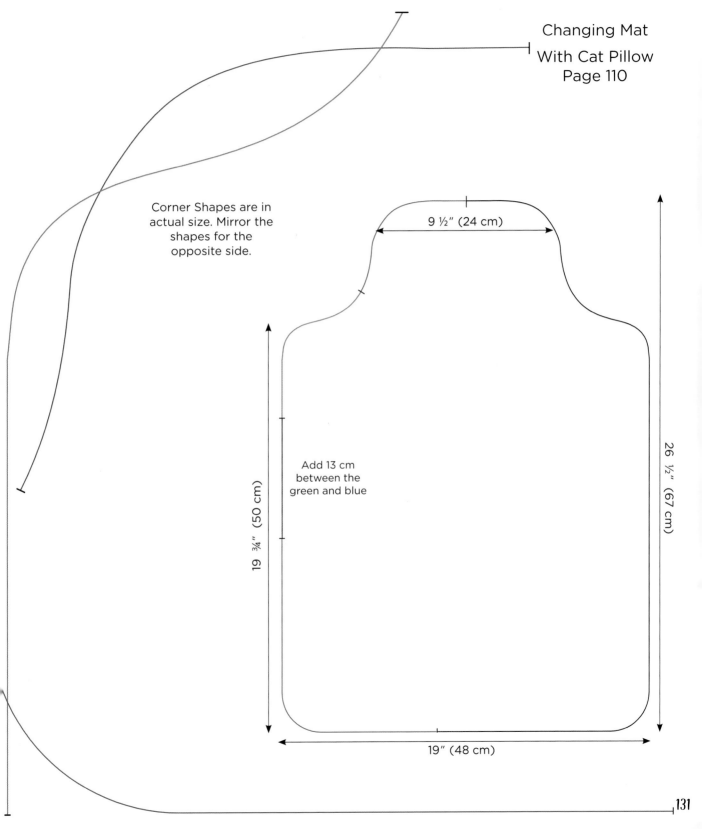

Corner Shapes are in
actual size. Mirror the
shapes for the
opposite side.

9 ½" (24 cm)

26 ½" (67 cm)

19 ¾" (50 cm)

Add 13 cm
between the
green and blue

19" (48 cm)

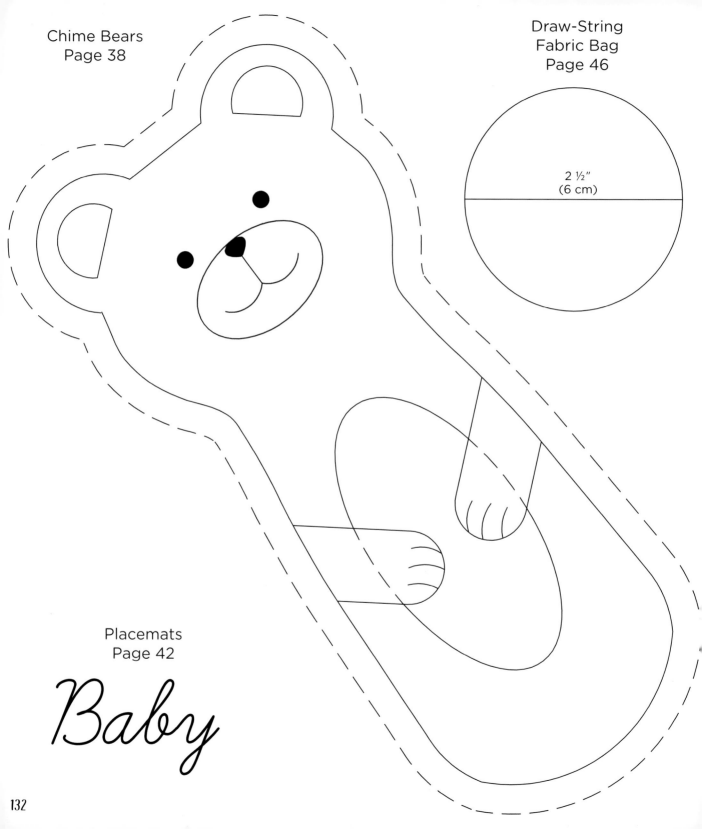

Chime Bears
Page 38

Draw-String
Fabric Bag
Page 46

2 ½″
(6 cm)

Placemats
Page 42

Baby

132

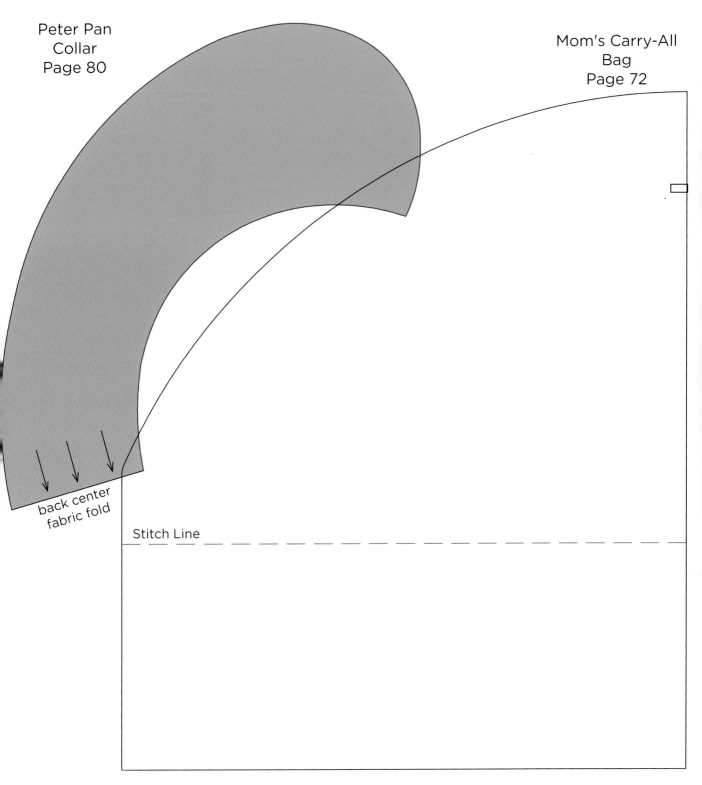

Peter Pan
Collar
Page 80

Mom's Carry-All
Bag
Page 72

back center
fabric fold

Stitch Line

133

House Wall
Organizer
Page 116

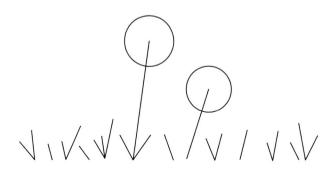

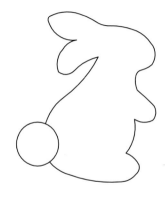

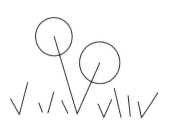

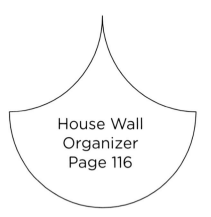

House Wall
Organizer
Page 116

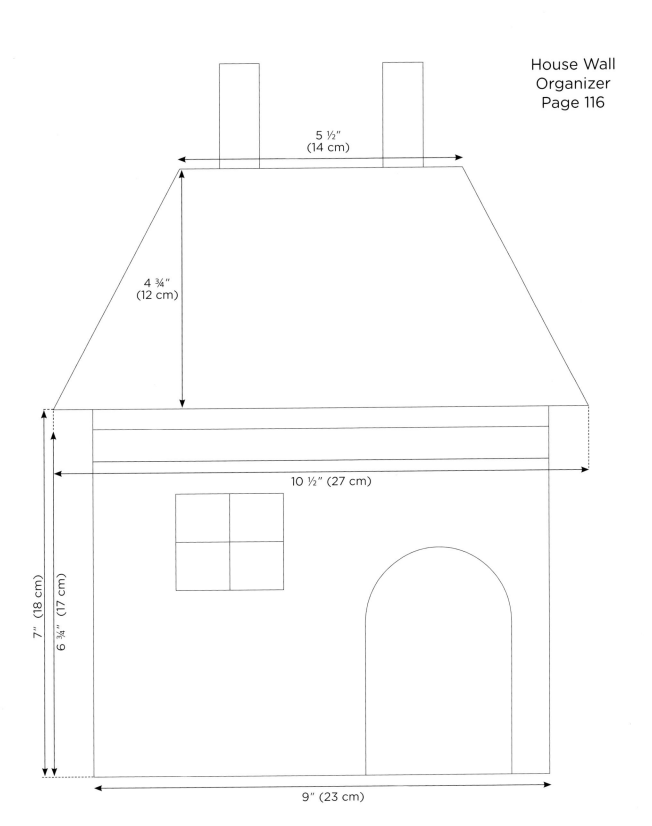

House Wall
Organizer
Page 116

5 ½"
(14 cm)

4 ¾"
(12 cm)

10 ½" (27 cm)

7" (18 cm)

6 ¾" (17 cm)

9" (23 cm)

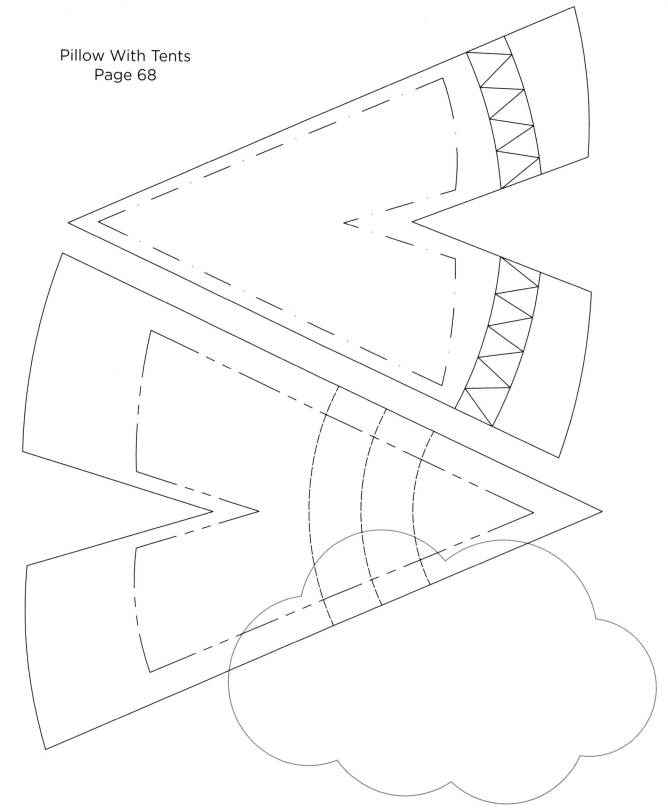

Pillow With Tents
Page 68

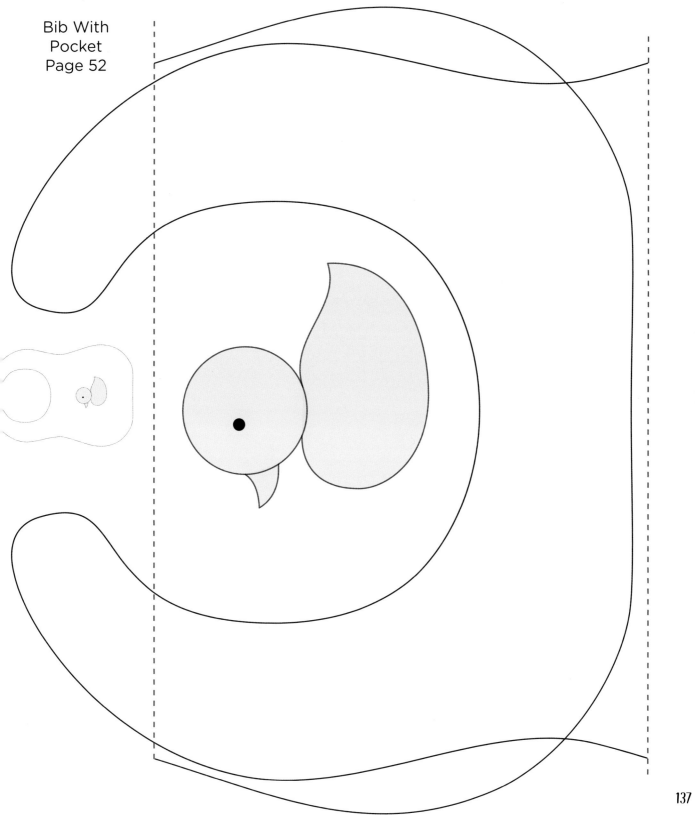

Bib With
Pocket
Page 52

137

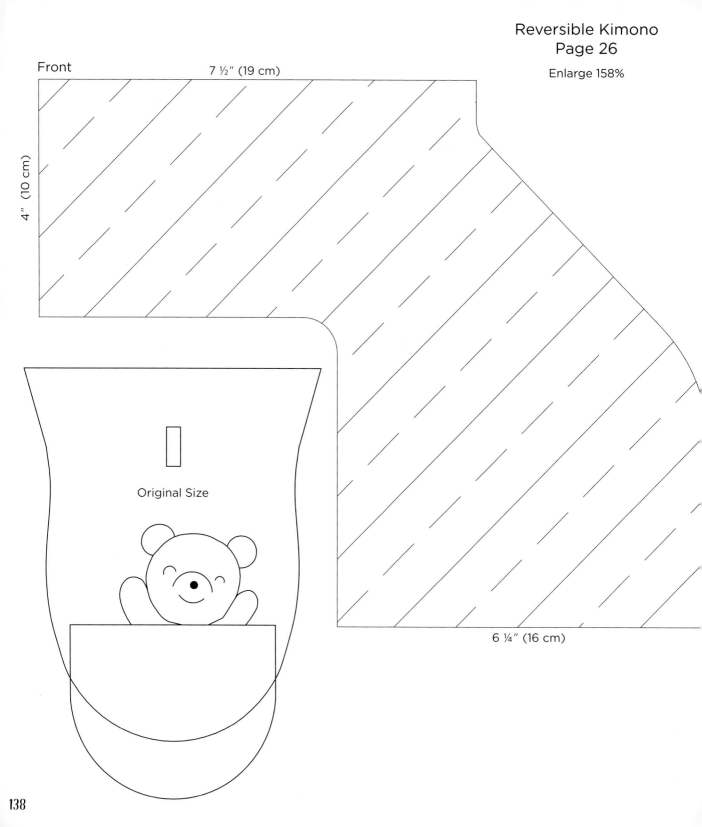

Front

7 ½" (19 cm)

4" (10 cm)

Reversible Kimono
Page 26

Enlarge 158%

Original Size

6 ¼" (16 cm)

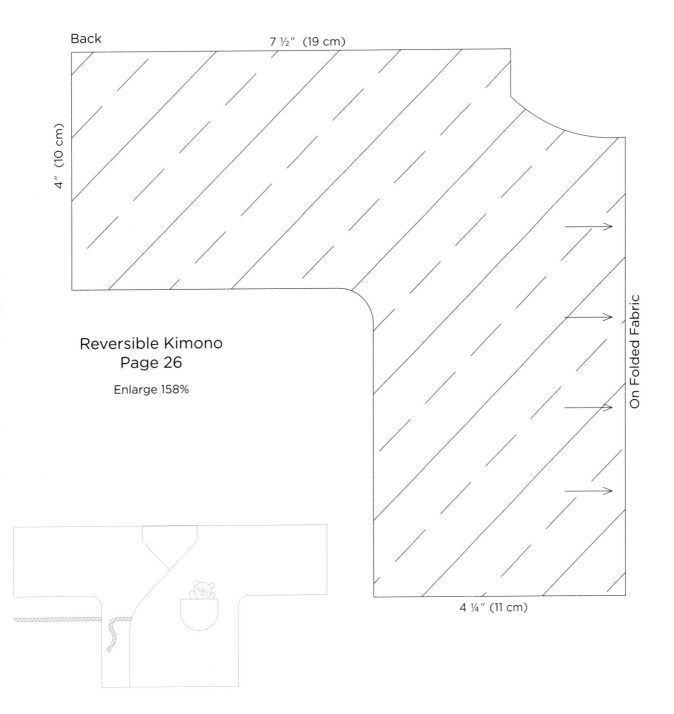

Back

7 ½" (19 cm)

4" (10 cm)

On Folded Fabric

Reversible Kimono
Page 26

Enlarge 158%

4 ¼" (11 cm)

Rabbit Soft Toy
Page 56

141

Playmat With Numbers
Page 106

Embroidered Burp Cloth
Set & Bag
Page 32

Patchwork Blanket
Page 122

143

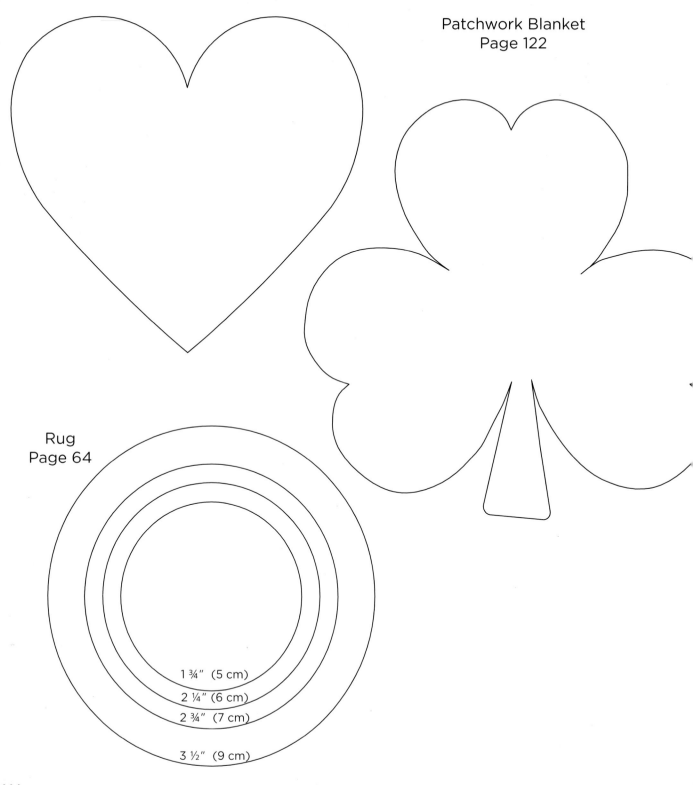

Patchwork Blanket
Page 122

Rug
Page 64

1 ¾" (5 cm)
2 ¼" (6 cm)
2 ¾" (7 cm)
3 ½" (9 cm)